BROWN BELT
SUDOKU™

Michael Rios

Sterling Publishing Co., Inc.
New York

CONTENTS

4 6 8 10 9 7 5 3

Martial Arts Sudoku and Brown Belt Sudoku
are trademarks of Sterling Publishing Co., Inc.

Published by Sterling Publishing Co., Inc.
387 Park Avenue South, New York, NY 10016
© 2005 by Michael Rios
Distributed in Canada by Sterling Publishing
c/o Canadian Manda Group, 165 Dufferin Street,
Toronto, Ontario, Canada M6K 3H6
Distributed in the United Kingdom by GMC Distribution Services,
Castle Place, 166 High Street, Lewes, East Sussex, England BN7 1XU
Distributed in Australia by Capricorn Link (Australia) Pty. Ltd.
P.O. Box 704, Windsor, NSW 2756, Australia

Manufactured in China
All rights reserved

Sterling ISBN-13: 978-1-4027-4023-7
ISBN-10: 1-4027-4023-9

For information about custom editions, special sales, premium and
corporate purchases, please contact Sterling Special Sales
Department at 800-805-5489 or specialsales@sterlingpub.com.

INTRODUCTION

To solve sudoku puzzles, all you need to know is this one simple rule:

Fill in the boxes so that each of the nine rows, each of the nine columns, and each of the nine 3×3 sections contain all the numbers from 1 to 9.

And that's all there is to it! Using these simple rules, let's see how far we get on this sample puzzle at right. (The letters at the top and left edges of the puzzle are for reference only; you won't see them in the regular puzzles.)

The first number that can be filled in is an obvious one: box EN is the only blank box in the center 3×3 section, and all the digits 1 through 9 are represented except for 5. EN must be 5.

	A	B	C	D	E	F	G	H	I
J									
K					2		1	8	4
L	9		5		7		2		6
M	1		4	3	9	2		7	
N				7		6			
O		7		1	4	8	9		2
P	3		2		6		8		5
Q	8	4	9		3				
R									

The next box is a little trickier to discover. Consider the upper left 3×3 section of the puzzle. Where can a 4 go? It can't go in AK, BK, or CK because row K already has a 4 at IK. It can't go in BJ or BL because column B already has a 4 at BQ. It can't go in CJ because column C already has a 4 at CM. So it must go in AJ.

Another box in that same section that can now be filled is BJ. A 2 can't go in AK, BK, or CK due to the 2 at EK. The 2 at GL rules out a 2 at BL. And the 2 at CP means that a 2 can't go in CJ. So BJ must contain the 2. It is worth noting that this 2 couldn't have been placed without the 4 at AJ in place. Many of the puzzles rely on this type of steppingstone behavior.

We now have a grid as shown.

Let's examine column A. There are four blank boxes in column A; in which blank box must the 2 be placed? It can't be AK because of the 2 in EK (and the 2 in BJ). It can't be AO because of the 2 in IO. It can't be AR because of the 2 in CP. Thus, it must be AN that has the 2.

	A	B	C	D	E	F	G	H	I
J	4	2							
K					2		1	8	4
L	9		5		7		2		6
M	1		4	3	9	2		7	
N				7	5	6			
O		7		1	4	8	9		2
P	3		2		6		8		5
Q	8	4	9		3				
R									

3

By the 9's in AL, EM, and CQ, box BN must be 9. Do you see how?

We can now determine the value for box IM. Looking at row M and then column I, we find all the digits 1 through 9 are represented but 8. IM must be 8.

This brief example of some of the techniques leaves us with the grid at right.

You should now be able to use what you learned to fill in CN followed by BL, then HL followed by DL and FL.

As you keep going through this puzzle, you'll find it gets easier as you fill in more. And as you keep working through the puzzles in this book, you'll find it gets easier and more fun each time. The final answer is shown below.

This book consists of 300 puzzles of hard level of difficulty.

—Michael Rios

	A	B	C	D	E	F	G	H	I
J	4	2							
K					2		1	8	4
L	9		5		7		2		6
M	1		4	3	9	2		7	8
N	2	9		7	5	6			
O		7		1	4	8	9		2
P	3		2		6		8		5
Q	8	4	9		3				
R									

	A	B	C	D	E	F	G	H	I
J	4	2	1	6	8	3	5	9	7
K	7	3	6	5	2	9	1	8	4
L	9	8	5	4	7	1	2	3	6
M	1	5	4	3	9	2	6	7	8
N	2	9	8	7	5	6	4	1	3
O	6	7	3	1	4	8	9	5	2
P	3	1	2	9	6	7	8	4	5
Q	8	4	9	2	3	5	7	6	1
R	5	6	7	8	1	4	3	2	9

1

			3	8		7		2
							1	
	1		4			5	6	
8	6							
		3	7	2	9	6		
							3	9
	4	8			2		5	
	3							
5		7		3	4			

2

	3		9			8		5
				3		6		
9							3	4
4				8	6			
2			3		4			1
			5	9				6
3	8							7
		4		5				
7		6			2		5	

3

	7		9					
8	2		4		3			
	4	9	5					
		8		7		2		6
		7				1		
2		4		3		9		
					2	7	1	
			6		5		9	8
					8		6	

4

8	4	9	6		5			
				2	4			
								5
	1		2			7	9	
6		7		3		5		8
	5	4			1		2	
1								
			8	1				
			9		3	4	8	1

5

		3						
		7	2	6			1	
	5						2	9
6		1			7	3		
3	4			2			6	8
		9	8			1		4
1	6						8	
	3			7	8	6		
						9		

6

5				6				
	9	8	3					5
6				7		9		
		4		1	3			
3		1		5		4		8
			2	8		7		
		5		2				1
8					1	3	4	
				3				2

7

5			7			4		
3	6			5			2	
		1	4		8			
8			5					
1	4			6			3	7
					4			1
			8		1	3		
	1			7			8	4
		6			3			9

8

				3		6		4
	6			4			3	1
		5	2					
4	1							
5		9	7		4	1		8
							2	9
				2	3			
9	5			1			8	
8		4	7					

9

		9	8					
					5	9		1
1				3			4	
3		7	5				9	4
		5				7		
4	1				6	5		8
	4			8				9
6		1	9					
					7	1		

10

7	2			6		8		
6			7			2		3
	1		2					
				1	2		6	
	7			8			4	
	9		3	7				
					3		2	
4		1			6			9
		8		4			3	6

	9		8		1			
2		5					7	
	3		7	2	6		9	
		9					5	
			3	4	7			
	2					8		
	8		9	1	4		6	
	7					1		9
			6		2		8	

	8		6	7				
			3			8		2
		3		4		1		
4						2	9	6
	7						8	
8	1	6						3
		4		8		9		
9		7			4			
				9	2		3	

9			3				5	
	3				5		2	9
4	2			8	1			
				9	4		6	
	4		2	3				
			4	1			3	6
8	1		5				4	
	6				9			2

				6		1		7
	9	5			4		3	
			8				4	6
		3				5	7	
	7						1	
	5	4				6		
7	6				1			
	8		7			3	9	
5		9		2				

1
5

8				3		2		6
	3			9				
	6		1		4			
	7	6				3		2
			4		7			
9		4				5	7	
			9		8		3	
				2			9	
3		5		7				8

1
6

7				3		6		
		8						5
		5				3	7	9
	4		6					8
6			2	1	9			3
9					4		2	
3	5	9				8		
8						4		
		4		8				2

	4			8	9			
9	8		7		5		2	
2		5	1					
		3						6
		6		1		8		
1						4		
					1	9		2
	5		4		6		3	7
			8	9			4	

4				6	9	5		
9	8							7
1		3	8					
3							9	
	9		2		8		5	
	1							2
					5	6		1
6							7	5
		5	1	2				3

		5	2	7				
							1	
		6	9	5		2		4
4				2			9	
9		1				3		6
	6			8				7
7		2		1	6	9		
	4							
				9	5	7		

		7	1		4	8		
						7		
	2		6				4	5
7					5	1		
	6	4				3	5	
		1	4					7
2	4				6		8	
		6						
		8	9		3	6		

					1		6	3
7	1				8			2
8				2			1	
				4	6			7
			3		7			
9			8	1				
	8			6				4
5			4				7	9
3	9		5					

					2			9
			9	4				3
1	6			3				
		4	3	2	5	9		
		5				1		
		8	7	9	1	2		
				6			2	8
4				7	3			
5			2					

		7	3			5	8	4
8	3							1
		6			7	3		
			1					
	5		2		3		4	
					9			
		8	6			7		
6							9	3
1	9	2			5	4		

					4		7	
		9	8					
1	8			6	7		5	9
	1	6						
3			7	4	5			1
						3	9	
7	3		5	9			8	6
					8	7		
	5		1					

	8			9		4	3	
5	6	3			8			
		7					5	
				2		1		
			9	3	4			
		2		7				
	1					3		
			7			8	9	1
	7	6		1			2	

5	6			4				
2				6	5	7	9	
							1	
		4	3	8				
	3		6		9		2	
				2	4	1		
	7							
	4	9	1	3				5
				9			4	2

2
7

			3		5		8	1
		7						
						9	4	6
		3			7			9
	1		6	3	2		7	
7			9			8		
5	6	8						
						5		
3	4		1		8			

2
8

		6	7			8		2
			6			9		
	1							4
			9		5	2	3	
	2		1	6	8		5	
	5	9	3		2			
1							2	
		5			3			
9		4			6	5		

4		3	6				7	
	5		9					2
					3		5	
8			3	2		7		4
				8				
7		4		6	5			8
	8		5					
2					8		1	
	7				4	9		3

2			8		4			
		8	3				2	6
9		1		6				
4		6			7			9
				3				
1			4			6		2
				2		8		5
6	2					8	7	
			5		1			4

Puzzle 3-1:

			5			3	8	
8					6		1	
6			9	4				
4		8				6		
	7		8	3	2		5	
		3				8		2
				8	1			9
	8		7					3
	6	9			3			

Puzzle 3-2:

	8	3					6	9
5					7	1		
9							2	
	1		2			8	9	
			3		6			
	2	8			1		5	
	3							4
		1	8					3
4	5					9	8	

3 / 3

	8	1				2		3
	3	2	4	5				
6		7			4		3	
			6	7	9			
	1		2			4		6
				8	6	7	5	
8		9				1	6	

3 / 4

								7
8					5	6	2	
3		5	2			9		
	5	3				8		9
4				8				2
7		9				1	4	
		2			4	5		3
	4	1	3					6
5								

9	1	3		7	8			
6		4		9		3		
8			3			9		
	5		9	1	2		7	
		1			6			4
		8		5		6		9
			2	6		1	5	8

			1			6	3	
	4	2	7				1	
5								9
3		4			7			6
		9		6		7		
1			9			8		4
2								7
	9				5	2	6	
	8	6			9			

	9				7			2
4		1				6		
	2		9	5				
	1			7		5		
8		5		1		2		4
		2		8			1	
				4	2		3	
		9				7		6
5			8				2	

			1	9		5		
		2						3
		8	6				4	7
3	5	9		7				
			8		6			
				5		4	3	1
1	9				8	2		
8						9		
		6		4	9			

4				2			8	7
	2			4	8			9
	8		7			5		
5				9			3	
				1				
	4			5				2
		4			5		9	
3			6	8			4	
9	7			3				5

		2	4			1	9	
							3	
	7			9	2			
3			7		9			4
	2			3			1	
7			5		1			6
			1	8			2	
	6							
	1	9			3	4		

4
1

1	5			3				8
							2	
		3		4	8		7	
		2		9			1	
	1	9				8	4	
	6			5		2		
	3		9	6		1		
	7							
9				2			3	4

4
2

	5		9		2		8	7
						1	3	
				7	1			
7				2	3			8
2								4
8			7	6				2
			6	3				
	7	8						
1	9		8		7		2	

7		4		8			5	3
	3					1		
		9	2			4		
9		7						
	1		5		9		3	
						5		8
		3			1	7		
		2					1	
5	7			3		8		9

6		4				8	5	7
	2	5						
			4	9				
5				7	4			3
9				5				2
8			1	2				9
			4	9				
						2	3	
4	1	3				9		5

8			3		4			
		9	1				7	5
	5					6		
6	2				9			
3		8		1		2		7
			8				9	6
		2					3	
5	1				6	8		
			7		2			1

	2			5	1	9	8	6
						3		
7	5				3	1		
			6					
2		9				6		4
					5			
		2	3				9	8
		8						
4	9	7	8	2			1	

			8	7		1	4	
			4		2		7	3
7		2			8	4		1
		6		1		7		
9		8	2			5		6
2	5		9		6			
	6	7		3	1			

5					9		8	3
2		9	1					
3				7	4		5	
						4		7
	5			1			3	
8		3						
	6		4	9				5
					2	9		4
4	9		5					1

4	9		1		8		3	
	1							7
6							5	
			4	1		2		9
	2			3			8	
5		4		8	9			
	4							1
1							4	
	8		9		1		6	5

1			9					8
		5		6				7
			7			9	2	6
	2					3		
3			8		6			9
		8					4	
5	3	1			9			
9				8		7		
8					5			1

	9						3	2
3		7						6
			4	1			9	
7	5			6				4
		6		3		1		
8				5			6	9
	7			2	8			
2						6		1
4	8						5	

			6	3			4	
					4			5
		4	5		2		1	
		6			7	4		
3	7			4			2	6
		5	8			7		
	6		3		8	5		
4			2					
	3			5	1			

5/3

		9			8			
1	5							
3					9	6	8	
		3		8	5		7	
9		4		2		8		1
	8		9	6		4		
	7	2	6					4
							2	3
			5			7		

5/4

4			1				2	
	3	2					8	
		5		8	6			9
				4			7	2
8								3
5	6			2				
2			9	1		3		
	1					2	6	
	5				2			8

5 5

5					7	1		
					4		8	6
2	8			6			5	
					3	9		1
			1		5			
3		8	4					
	5			1			9	4
1	7		5					
		2	6					8

5 6

		1		5	9	2		
	9							
7			1		4			
9		3		2				5
1			9	8	3			4
2				4		3		7
			7		5			6
							8	
		7	4	9		5		

5/7

3			9		6	1	4	
		1	8			3	5	
							9	6
				4	9			
		2				6		
			6	7				
8	1							
	7	3			1	5		
	9	4	2		8			3

5/8

		3						
8	2							6
4					1		7	2
		9	4		6		5	
		2		7		8		
	7		3		5	4		
1	3		2					8
2							9	1
						2		

59

4	7		1				8	
				4		9		
		5	2					
7	8			3				2
3			7	2	5			9
9				8			1	3
					7	4		
		9		6				
	1				4		2	5

60

			4		3		6	8
5			7	9		4		
						5	3	
	4		8	3				
		5				2		
				4	7		9	
	3	6						
		1		7	9			2
7	9		6		8			

8		1			3	9		6
				1		8	2	3
		9		6				
5	1							
		3		7		4		
							1	5
				2		3		
6	8	5		4				
3		4	1			5		8

9	8		3					4
							7	6
			6			3	9	
			2		8	4		
5		9				1		2
		8	7		1			
	4	5			3			
6	1							
3					2		4	1

9							7	
							4	8
8				5	4	3	2	
			8		1		6	
5		4				1		3
	3		9		5			
	2	5	3	9				6
1	9							
	6							7

			4		9	5		3
3					6			
2		4		7			8	
5			1					
6		1		4		2		7
					5			9
	6			9		3		1
			7					5
7		8	5		3			

		6	9				7	
3			4		6			
8	9		2	1				
1			6				3	
2				7				8
	7				4			5
				4	1		9	3
			8		9			4
	4				5	1		

1					7		2	
		7	5	3				
2	9	3					7	
7			3					8
			7	5	9			
6					8			1
	1					2	4	9
				8	5	3		
	3		9					7

						1		2
9		5			8	3		
			9	6	3			
1	7				2			
8		9		5		6		1
			8				7	3
			3	8	6			
		6	4			7		9
5		3						

3	9				4			
2		5		6			7	
	4				2		3	
	1	4	5					
9				7				1
					1	3	8	
	2		1				9	
	3			8		2		7
			3				6	5

7	1			3	6			2
		2			9			7
				2			5	3
		8						
	6		3	8	2		1	
						2		
1	8			6				
5			2			6		
9			8	4			3	5

4							9	
		6		7				3
		9	4					1
					1	7	5	
9			5	2	7			8
	1	7	9					
1					4	5		
3				9		4		
	8							6

7/1

1			7			4		
		6						7
7			9				1	2
8	9			5			2	
			2		7			
	1			9			6	3
6	2				3			9
4						2		
		5			9			4

7/2

2			7			9	4	3
		1					5	
9	4						1	
					8		7	
		5	1	7	3	4		
	8		5					
	7						2	9
	2					1		
8	1	4			2			7

7/3

		4	8	9				5
					5			
						7	1	9
		7				2		6
	5		6	7	4		3	
4		6				9		
8	7	5						
			3					
3				2	8	1		

7/4

				4			6	2
						1		
	6			5				4
	4	2			5			6
	7	6	4		1	3	9	
5			9			2	4	
2				8			3	
		9						
7	5			6				

		2			5	1	3	
	3	9	7	8				2
	8			2		6		
1		3						
						2		4
		4		7			9	
9				4	6	7	2	
	1	6	2			8		

8								1
				5				3
	4		8		1		5	2
9		6	4					
	8			2			4	
					3	8		5
7	2		5		4		9	
5				8				
3								4

7 / 7

		5	1				4	
		2						1
9			5	4		8	7	
3				5		2		
				3				
		1		7				6
	5	4		8	7			3
7						9		
	9				4	6		

7 / 8

	3			8	4			
	1							5
9	4			1	3			
					2		8	
5		2		9		1		7
	8		4					
			1	6			2	8
7							9	
			2	4			7	

	3				8	4		
9				6			5	8
8		2						
				7	8			
2	1			3			7	9
		7	8					
						2		1
3	7			9				5
		5	3				9	

2			8					
	8		2					9
7		9		1		8		
	9		1	8		7		
	5						1	
		6		4	2		3	
		8		6		3		2
3					8		5	
					1			6

7	3							
9			6		7			
	2		4			6	7	
				4		8	1	
6			5		3			4
	8	7		1				
	6	4			5		2	
			3		2			7
							3	1

	7	9				4		
	1		3			5		
			6			9		8
8		1			4		9	
	9			2			8	
	2		8			7		1
7		4			3			
		2			8		5	
		5				1	3	

8 / 3

5			3	7	2		6	
				8				9
	1	8					7	
			2			3		5
			6	3	7			
4		2			5			
	9					4	8	
8				9				
	2		7	6	8			1

8 / 4

								4
4	1		2			6		7
			6	5	1			
	8			4			3	
3			6		8			1
	2			9			6	
		2	5	7				
8		4			1		5	9
1								

						9	5	
			4			7	3	1
4		5					6	
	6		9	5			7	
			1		8			
	3			2	7		1	
	8					6		2
5	4	9			2			
	7	6						

4	9			3	1			
5					9		1	
			7					
		9	8				5	3
	1	4		6		8	7	
3	5				7	1		
					2			
	7		9					5
			3	8			6	1

8/7

7				9		6		
	4	2	6			5		
6								4
		1			2		9	
4			9		7			8
	9		5			2		
2								1
		6			3	4	7	
		5		8				3

8/8

2	9		4					5
1	4							3
			8				1	
	2		7		6		4	
		3		9		7		
	7		3		2		6	
	8				4			
9							7	4
3					7		2	9

5		8						
	4							
2			1	6	5		4	
	2	6			7	1		
	8		2	1	3		6	
		7	9			2	3	
	1		5	3	9			6
							1	
						4		7

	9	6		4				
8		2						
	3				6			8
		4		2	5			
3	1			9			5	7
			8	7		1		
6			4				1	
						3		5
				5		9	8	

6						4		
				1	8		5	
7		5	3			9		
4			8	7			2	
			4		9			
	2			3	6			4
		9			2	8		3
	6		1	5				
		7						6

			7	8		1	4	
1		2						
							3	5
		8			3		6	
9			8	7	2			3
	1		5			4		
3	7							
						9		6
	5	6		2	8			

		4	8				5	
	7							
			4	7	3			9
6		5	2			3		
1	3						9	2
		9			7	1		6
2			7	1	8			
							4	
	9					5	8	

			6				4	
2	9	5			4		1	
		3						2
	1	4		5				
9				8				4
				2		7	6	
7						2		
	3		7			4	9	1
	4				3			

	6		3	1			4	7
	2				7			
9					5		8	1
			6					
	4		2	9	8		3	
					3			
8	9		5					3
			9				1	
7	3			8	4		9	

						2		
		9			5	6	1	3
		2	8			7	9	
				6			8	
1			7	5	2			4
	2			8				
	4	8			6	1		
5	3	6	1			4		
		1						

8		5			7		6	
	3		1		6			
6		4			2		8	3
4	5							
				7				
							3	9
7	8		4			5		6
			5		8		7	
	9		7			1		8

				7		9	1	
						7		5
	2	8			9			
	5	4	7			2	9	
				4				
	6	3			8	4	5	
			2			8	6	
6		9						
	3	7		9				

9			2	5	8			
	2		1			7	9	
		3						2
1	5				2			
	3			1			6	
			6				2	3
6						4		
	7	1			6		5	
			8	3	7			9

6	7			5	2	9		8
8	9				4			
		2			6			
1		7					8	
				6				
	5					2		3
			3			4		
			8				5	2
7		3	6	4			9	1

1	6							
3			7		9			
4		7				1		
		5		7	2		4	
			5		6			
	3		1	4		9		
		2				4		3
			6		3			2
							8	7

	9	1		6	3			
2			5		7	1		
	7		4				8	5
	5						6	
1	8				2		9	
		7	1		6			8
			2	9		4	1	

	8				7	5		2
	3		9					8
							1	
		6		9	8			
		9				2		
			1	3		4		
	9							
6					2		5	
8		1	3				6	

		8			9		4	
		3			5		7	
1			4					
9	2			5				
		4	3		6	1		
				8			5	2
					2			9
	7		6			3		
	8		7			4		

105

	2			9		5	6	
			2	1				
	8	3			6			
6						3	7	9
3	1	8						4
			4			9	5	
				3	9			
	4	1		2			8	

106

	6		1					
							8	
7		2	5	8	3			
3	9				6			2
2								6
6			4				1	7
			7	1	5	4		3
	4							
					9		6	

4								9
				9			7	
					7	3	8	1
		3			6	1		
	7		4		9		2	
		9	2			5		
2	3	6	5					
	8			1				
9								3

9		4					5	
			2		3		7	
					5	3		
2		8	5					9
			3		4			
6					9	1		8
		5	9					
	7		8		6			
	2					8		6

7							2	
			3			4		6
5			9		7			1
2			8			9	3	
	3	5			1			2
3			7		4			5
1		4			8			
	8							3

9	7							
8				2		9	5	
			5				6	
5	1				4			7
		3				5		
2			3				1	6
	4				8			
	9	2		7				3
							9	1

111

	8					7	4	6
		1	7		4			
	6				9			
	5	4	9					7
7					5	1	8	
			6				3	
			8		7	5		
2	4	3					7	

112

4			5					1
		7		1	3	4		
	3			2				
	5	8			2			
				7				
			9			7	8	
				4			6	
		4	2	3		9		
9					7			2

60

		7						
			6		3			
5	8			2	1			
3			7				8	4
		2		9		6		
8	4				2			5
			3	4			6	7
			9		8			
						9		

			3					5
	3		4				6	1
5					2	9		
			6			4		
2			7		9			6
		8			3			
		9	5					7
6	2				4		8	
8					1			

			6			3	4	
	3	9					8	
		6				7		
			5	4			1	
	1			2			7	
	8			3	9			
		5				6		
	6					9	2	
	9	1			8			

8	9				7		5	6
		5				4		
	2							
9					1	7	2	
			8		9			
	3	6	2					5
							4	
		3				9		
2	7		6				8	3

3	7	8	6					
		1		9				4
						7		
9				7		4	8	
				5				
	5	3		1				6
		7						
4				3		6		
					2	9	5	1

		5			8		3	
			9	5		6		
8	3							
6				2			7	9
2								8
4	5			1				6
							1	2
		7		4	5			
	2		6			8		

8		4	9				1	
			6		1		2	8
				8		9		
6							3	7
1	7							5
		2		5				
7	5		1		4			
	9				2	7		3

	1	6	2				3	
3			5					
					9		7	
	3			6			1	4
			4		5			
1	2			9			8	
	7		1					
					4			6
	9				8	2	4	

1	9					4		
5			1		6	7		
6				5				
			7		1	9		
				2				
		4	8		3			
				6				1
		3	2		4			8
		5					6	4

		1	3	6				
2		8	5					3
9							7	
		9	1				5	7
6	4				8	1		
	5							1
8					7	4		9
				1	2	7		

Puzzle 1:

		9						
3			4			9	5	
	1	7						
5			9	1				6
		2	6		5	1		
1				4	7			8
						3	7	
	7	8			9			4
						8		

Puzzle 2:

		7	2				6	
					7			5
4	6	2	1					3
2						5		
				4				
		8						1
3					9	7	2	6
5			6					
	4				1	8		

					7		4	
1							2	
			9	1			3	
5				4		3		
8	2		3		1		9	6
		9		5				7
	8			3	2			
	5							8
	7		8					

					9		5	
	4						8	
7	8	6		4				
		1		6	3			
2		8				5		3
			9	8		2		
			3			1	4	5
	6						9	
	7		1					

8	7			5			1	
	5							6
		1				4		
					4	9	3	1
				6				
9	4	2	5					
		4				3		
5							8	
	1			8			7	4

	1			4		9	8	
	7						6	
3		4			5	2		
2				1			4	
	6			5				8
		3	8			6		5
	8						1	
	2	5		7			3	

Puzzle 129:

	3	9						
6					2			
		7			8		1	
	9			1		2		
1			5		6			7
		3		7			8	
	4		3			7		
			8					2
						6	9	

Puzzle 130:

				3	7			2
					1		6	
	5		6			1		
5	9			6		4		
	3						9	
		2		9			3	1
		8			3		5	
	6		2					
7			4	1				

		7						
	9		8		3			
6				1		4	9	
		1		3	7		2	9
2	6		4	5		1		
	1	3		8				4
			1		5		3	
						5		

8			7	9				
					2	5	6	7
	3				5			
1			3			9		
				1				
		2			4			3
			9				1	
4	1	7	6					
				5	1			2

133

			1		4		2	
				7			1	
6				8				3
	1	4				3		
	8		3		9		7	
		2				9	6	
8				1				9
	2			4				
	3		2		5			

134

				8	1		5	
		1	5			6	2	
7					6			
	3							8
8		9				5		2
6							9	
			8					7
	4	7			2	1		
	1		9	6				

	4		2				7	
8			6				3	
3			5	8				
		2					8	4
4								2
6	8					1		
				5	2			1
	9				8			5
	6				7		9	

	4		9					2
	2				5	4	9	
	3		4					
						3	4	
			7	6	9			
	5	7						
					8		5	
	9	3	6				2	
6					2		1	

	7			1	4			2
		3		9				
		9	2			3		6
		8			2			3
3			7			4		
4		7			9	5		
				5		9		
2			1	7			3	

				4				
		1		7	3			4
	4	7					5	2
	8						7	9
		9				5		
1	7						6	
3	5					1	9	
8			1	6		2		
				8				

			7		6			2
				9			7	
	4	1			2	5		
	8		6					
6				8				4
					1		5	
		6	5			8	2	
	5			1				
1			9		4			

		6						
	3		1				6	5
				8	9		1	
2	9				4			
		5		2		1		
			8				7	9
	7		5	3				
5	4				2		3	
					9			

Puzzle 141

				7		4		
	8						3	1
		5	6			2		
				2			8	3
	3			5			9	
7	4			6				
		3			4	8		
9	1						5	
		8		9				

Puzzle 142

					6	3		
6						4	8	
3					4			9
		9	8	5			2	
4								1
	1			4	9	7		
8			7					5
	9	5						3
		7	1					

7				5				
3	2	9				6		
		1	6			4		
8			1			7	3	
	5	4			8			2
		8			6	9		
		7				3	5	4
			2					7

9					3	6	2	
			9	1	7	3		
				4		1	5	
	3					2		
		5					4	
	4	8		9				
		3	6	5	2			
	2	6	4					5

	7	2		3		4		
		3						
	8	5			7			6
4			5		3			
	1						8	
			7		8			9
8			1			9	2	
						7		
		7		2		8	3	

9		1				8		5
8	5							
6					2			
	9		6			5		1
2								4
3		5			9		6	
			4					8
							1	6
5		4				2		3

			4				3	
4		1		6	3			
8		5						
		6	7	3			4	
				2				
	7			8	4	2		
						5		6
			2	9		1		7
	9				6			

3		2		7			5	8
	8	4						
1					6		3	
	6	9						
			7		1			
						7	6	
	5		9					6
						1	8	
4	3			1		2		9

	8			5	1			9
			9					
	3	2	8				4	
		7		6				
	9	6				4	3	
				3		1		
	7					2	8	5
					7			
2			3	9			6	

	6					1		
			3	9				
			5	6			4	2
	3				8		9	6
	7						8	
6	2		7				3	
9	8			5	3			
				1	2			
		2					1	

151

	1	9		2		5		
		5			4		3	8
				9				
	4							
	3		8		1		7	
							4	
				7				
7	6		3			1		
		8		1		7	9	

152

		6			9			
			6	2				
		2		1		8		6
	2				3	9		8
6								3
7		1	5				2	
8		7		3		1		
				7	2			
			1			5		

153

			9					
2				8	3	1		
					5	8		6
5				3				
	2	3	6		8	9	7	
				1				2
4		8	1					
		1	3	5				7
					7			

154

	1					3		
			5	8	3			
	6	9						
	4				9	2		
	7		3	1	6		9	
		8	2				5	
						8	3	
			7	6	4			
		4					1	

		1						7
					8		4	1
9			3				2	
		7				1		6
			2	5	6			
6		9				4		
	6				5			4
2	1		4					
3						8		

	5				8	2	6	
	7	8			4			
			1			5		
2			6				3	
				2				
	8				9			4
		4			7			
			4			3	9	
	6	2	3				7	

				5				
	3					7		9
		8	6					
7	8				2			6
	5	2		6		3	9	
1			7				8	2
					1	9		
2		9					4	
				3				

		7					3	
	3	4			6	2		
5			3				1	
	8	2	5		3			
			4		8	9	5	
	2				5			8
		3	6			1	9	
	6					4		

159

							2	8
	6				1	9		3
					3	5		
2	7		5				1	
	3						4	
	1				7		8	9
		4	6					
6		7	2				9	
5	9							

160

	3		6			8	2	4
			3	5				
	9	8						
6		7						3
			7		2			
2						1		8
						9	5	
			7	6				
3	8	5			1		4	

161

		3		2	1			
		8			5	4	2	
			6					
2	5			6		9		
6								5
		1		7			3	4
					7			
	9	6	1			8		
			3	9		5		

162

	7		4	9				5
4	5						6	
			2					8
				3	2			
	6			8			9	
			9	4				
3					8			
	8						2	6
1				7	9		4	

6		1		4		8		
	4				2			9
	3				7		6	
			2	6				7
9			7	5				
	7		5				9	
8			3				2	
		4		9		7		8

5		7						
8	3			4	5			
2		4					1	
				5	4		7	
		1				5		
	5		8	3				
	8					2		9
			6	2			5	3
						6		7

		2			3		7	
		5	7				8	4
		7	1					
	9				2			6
				9				
1			5				4	
					6	3		
2	5				7	4		
	7		4			6		

6		7	3	4		8		
			8			4		
				5			9	
			5	7			2	
	2						3	
	8			3	4			
	9			2				
		6			5			
		4		1	6	9		3

				3			1	
			9		6		7	3
6				1			8	
9		1			4			
8								4
			5			3		7
	1			7				9
2	6		3		9			
	4			5				

		6		8				1
						2	9	
				7	6		3	
	8				9		5	
		2	3		7	8		
	5		8				1	
	7		5	6				
	6	8						
1				2		7		

2	8		7					
3		4						
		1				3	6	
			5					3
4	2		8		7		1	5
9					2			
	4	6				2		
						6		7
					8		4	1

3				7	6		8	1
		9			1			4
	5						7	
			5					3
				4				
6					7			
	7						2	
8			7			1		
5	4		3	9				7

171

8				5		6	7	4
				2	6		1	3
						2		
			3					2
		6				9		
7				6				
		5						
6	8		5	7				
4	7	3		1				5

172

		3	9		5			
	6	8						2
1			6					
			7					5
	2		1	3	8		9	
9				4				
					4			8
5						6	3	
			3		2	7		

173

	9			6	3			7
3	2		9					
		5			7			
						6		1
	3	1				5	4	
2		4						
			7			2		
					1		7	8
1			5	3			9	

174

	6				5	7		
		3				5		2
		8	4					
				6	7			4
9				3				1
7			5	8				
					3	6		
4		2				1		
		7	1				3	

	3		2				5	9
4		2			7			8
			8					
2							7	4
	9						2	
7	6							5
				2				
8			3			6		7
9	5				4		8	

						1	9	
							4	3
		2	5		4			
		7	4				1	
9		6		3		5		2
	3				9	7		
			1		2	6		
7	5							
	2	8						

		3	6					
							5	7
	4				5	9		
		6	4		9	2		
1				2				8
		8	5		6	7		
		4	1				8	
3	5							
					3	4		

4	3		2					
					4			8
		6	7		1			
9	5		3			8		
			1		5			
		1			8		6	7
			4		7	2		
7			6					
					9		1	5

2	5				6			8
	1	6			3			
				9		2		
7		3		1				
	2						5	
				7		1		4
		8		3				
			8			9	6	
9			1				7	3

					3		9	2
8	2				4	6		7
		6						4
			7		9			
	4						8	
			1		2			
9						7		
4		3	6				5	1
7	5		8					

Puzzle 181

		6	5				8	
		6	5				8	
8	1			7			4	2
		3	6			7		
9			1		4			3
		5			8	4		
4	9			2			3	5
	6				5	9		

Puzzle 182

4			2				1	
				6				2
		2	5		8	3		6
	1							
	5	9				6	2	
							8	
9		5	3		6	1		
1				7				
	3				4			8

183

1				5		8		
2							3	
	3							5
		6		7	1	4		
		1	5		9	3		
		9	2	8		7		
5							7	
	9							4
		8		3				9

184

			6	1			3	7
					3			5
8						6		4
6	9						1	
				5				
	2						9	3
3		6						8
7			4					
2	5			8	7			

185

5					4		9	
3								1
2						3	4	
	8	4	3		5			
			9		7			
			6		2	8	1	
	6	5						2
7								8
	9		8					6

186

1							4	
5		2	7		8			
	3							
			9	2		6	3	
	6			3			5	
	1	7		8	5			
							6	
			4		3	8		2
	7							9

Puzzle 187

				8	7	1	2	
	1							7
						3		
2					1		7	
	3	1				4	8	
	6		9					2
		7						
8							5	
	4	9	7	6				

Puzzle 188

			8		3	1		
							7	
2	3	4			7	6		
3	6				4			
			7		2			
			3				9	6
		2	9			8	4	5
	5							
		9	2		6			

	1		8			7	5	
6		5	9			1		
		3						
2				1				
	4			9			6	
				4				8
						5		
		6			9	2		1
	2	9			4		8	

		7				8		4
3	5	9						
	2		3		6			
			9	7				1
1								5
4				2	5			
			4		8		2	
						3	1	8
9		6				4		

						6		
2	5			1	9	8		
			5	4			7	1
	7		2					5
9					7		8	
3	1			5	2			
		7	4	9			3	6
		9						

	7	1			4			
			3			8		
					5		6	
2	5				6		9	
9				4				8
	4		8				7	3
	9		1					
		2			7			
			5			7	2	

						6	5	4
	1	2			5	9		
			8					7
							8	6
			2	8	3			
1	4							
7					6			
		5	1			2	7	
4	8	9						

8	2			4				
			6			1		
		3		2	8			
5		6		3		4		
		8				9		
		4		7		6		8
			9	8		5		
		5			2			
				1			3	7

195

		9		4				
5						6		1
	1		6		5		8	
					2	7		
9		4				5		8
		3	1					
	4		9		3		5	
6		7						2
				1		3		

196

		3		8		7	4	
			4				2	
			5					9
		5	1					8
2		4				5		7
9					5	3		
6					8			
	2				6			
	1	7		3		2		

		8					7	4
	4							6
6		2			3	9		
			9		8			3
4								8
3			6		1			
		1	3			2		9
8							6	
9	7					8		

6		3		5	8		7	
							3	
4			7			9		
		6		9				
2			8		5			6
				2		8		
		5			2			3
	9							
	8		3	7		4		5

						4	8	
	6				8	5		2
	3		6					7
		1		2			9	
6								4
	2			7		1		
9					1		7	
1		8	5				6	
	5	6						

		5		9		8		6
7	1		4				9	
		7	5			2		
	4		8		3		1	
		9			1	5		
	2				5		6	7
4		8		6		1		

1		4						
				9				
	2		6	8	4			7
5	8					7		6
			7		5			
9		6					1	3
8			2	4	1		7	
				3				
						9		8

1	8		9	6	5			
2					7		3	
7		4						
								9
9	1						6	4
8								
						4		8
	9		1					5
			6	9	2		1	7

203

			1				4	
						6		2
	1	7	4				5	8
5			6			9		
			9		7			
		3			4			1
6	3				2	5	8	
4		9						
	5				8			

204

		3	6					
	2	6	9				8	
		9	3				6	
		2		1			9	
8								4
	1			7		6		
	7				3	4		
	9				8	3	5	
					4	1		

Puzzle 205

			9			7	8	
		6	2					
				7	3	9		4
4	2						9	
6								1
	7						5	3
5		1	8	4				
					9	1		
	6	4			7			

Puzzle 206

5	3				7			
						3	7	9
			2				8	
		2	6	5				
3	4						5	1
			8	1	9			
	7				2			
6	1	4						
			4				1	8

	2							
5	1		3					
	4		9			2	6	
					7	3	1	
		2				7		
	6	9	5					
	8	4			2		7	
					1		9	4
							3	

	9	5	4	3		2		
							9	7
6						4		
			1	9			5	
8								2
	1			4	2			
		7						8
3	2							
		4		2	1	5	3	

7			8					
	1	5						
	6				9	5		1
1	5					4		
	3		6		4		1	
		7					5	3
9		8	4				6	
						7	3	
					2			4

	7						9	
						3	7	
6		5			1			
8			5					2
	2	4		6		7	3	
5					4			9
			9			1		7
	4	6						
	3						6	

9	3			1			7	
7	5							
				8			3	4
1	6	2			9			
			1			9	8	6
6	2			3				
							4	3
	9			5			1	8

7		2						
	9					8		6
			3		5	9		
2		7			9			
8		5				4		2
			4			1		8
		6	2		7			
4		1					5	
						7		1

213

8	9	7	2					
4			5				8	
5								4
				2	3	5	1	
	2	5	1	7				
7								8
	1				2			7
					6	1	4	9

214

				1			6	
		4	7					
5	8	1			9		4	
				4			2	
7	6						8	5
	4			8				
	1		4			7	3	9
					3	2		
	5			6				

		5			1	8		
9				4	3			
4	8		5					
	1					2		
		2	7		5	1		
		9					8	
					8		7	9
			3	9				4
		6	1			5		

8				5			4	9
				3			1	
9			8					
	2	4						1
		7		6		3		
5						2	6	
					4			7
	8			9				
4	7			1				5

4	3		6			5		
				5	4	1		
	1							
			4			8	9	
	9		7		3		5	
	4	8			5			
							2	
		7	9	3				
		9			7		8	6

8	9				4			
			3	6				
	2	7					5	
		1	2		5	8		
		2				3		
		4	6		8	2		
	5					1	4	
			5	7				
			9				2	6

7		6				3		
							2	
		2	8				7	5
		1			6	7		
5			4		7			8
		9	5			1		
1	9				8	5		
	6							
		7				9		3

7	1	5			6	3		
				7				
2	3		8					
1			2				5	
			4		7			
	9				1			2
					4		7	9
				9				
		7	3			1	8	5

2
2
1

			8					
	2					1	3	8
			4	6	2			
		1			8		7	5
			3		5			
3	9		1			2		
			7	5	6			
7	1	9					5	
					1			

2
2
2

	6			9				
		9		3	8		7	
		3						4
		4		6			3	
8	9						1	7
	5			1		4		
1						6		
	4		1	5		2		
				4			8	

3	8		5	4		7	2	
		1			2			
			9				5	
	4							
		3	8		7	6		
							8	
	2			7				
			4			1		
	7	8		3	1		6	9

8					6	7		4
3	7							
			3		2			
6		1				2		
	8			3			1	
		5				9		7
			5		8			
							4	9
7		2	4					6

3		7			9		1	
6			3		4			
5		2						
			7	9		6		
2								1
		1		8	6			
						3		8
			8		2			4
	6		4			9		7

	7			1			2	3
			8			6		1
	1				4	9		
						8		
9		8				5		6
		4						
		5	9				3	
7		9			2			
2	4			3			8	

227

2							8	4
	4				7	9		2
		6	8			5		
							7	
			9	1	3			
	2							
		3			6	1		
6		9	7				5	
7	1							8

228

	4		3				8	2
	6	5		9				7
		9						
9				1		2		
			9		6			
		4		8				5
						3		
3				2		4	7	
1	7				8		6	

3			2			1		9
				9	7			
	7		1					3
6				5		9		
1								4
		3		1				2
4					6		2	
			8	7				
9		8			2			6

				6	7			1
								9
8	2		5					
		2	4				9	
1		9		5		2		4
	5				6	8		
					3		5	6
7								
4			2	1				

2
3
1

3					8			
	2				6		4	
	9			5		8		1
1						7		
5			8		1			9
		2						3
2		3		7			6	
	6		5				3	
			2					8

2
3
2

						9		2
		2	9	6				
	9		7		5		8	
6						4	7	1
3	4	8						5
	2		1		3		6	
				9	7	8		
4		3						

				1				
	6						5	1
				6		7		9
	5		7			3	1	
7		2				8		5
	3	4			5		6	
8		7		5				
3	9						4	
				2				

8			3					5
5			6	1			3	
3						4		
				3	2	9		
		7				5		
		2	4	8				
		4						3
	8			6	3			9
1					7			8

2 3 5

				3	8	1		
				9			7	3
4	8		5			9		
		2						4
				8				
1						7		
		1			7		2	9
6	7			4				
		8	6	1				

2 3 6

				2			8	1
			7					9
				8	4			6
	6	2	3		5			
	7						2	
			2		6	9	3	
4			1	5				
7					8			
5	9			6				

2 3 7

7		6						
		4	8			7		1
				7	6			
2		7						4
3			1		2			7
8						6		3
			5	6				
1		9			3	5		
						9		8

2 3 8

				9				2
3		6		8			4	
					6		5	3
8				6		1		
			2		1			
		1		4				7
9	7		4					
	8			1		5		4
6				3				

Puzzle 239

	5		3		7	4		
9				6				2
1								
6	4			9			2	8
3	8			1			6	5
								3
8				3				1
		3	6		4		9	

Puzzle 240

	6			3			4	5
			5	2			7	
	7							
2						5		7
		3	9		1	8		
4		1						9
							8	
	1		2	4				
8	4			7			6	

				3				
	8		6	1		7	4	
1			7			8	2	
4								6
			8		2			
9								8
	1	3			9			5
	5	4		2	6		3	
				8				

					4	2		6
8				6				
7			8					
		3		1			7	
	9	2		3		4	1	
	1			9		8		
					6			3
				2				1
3		1	9					

3		1						
	2				5			1
7						5	6	
8			2	7				9
	4						1	
2				1	4			3
	6	7						2
1			8				9	
						4		5

		6	5				7	2
	1						9	
	8			6				
	6	5			2			
4			8		1			7
			3			2	5	
				2			4	
	2						3	
6	9				7	8		

7			9			1		
3	8	4				7		
					6		8	
			1	4	2			
	2						4	
			6	7	5			
	4		2					
		9				4	3	6
		5			9			2

3	9			4				
			1		2	7	5	
								8
6	1		9				7	
				8				
	8				6		2	9
2								
	6	4	2		3			
				1			4	5

2			8				1	
4		3				2		
			5	1			3	
					9		4	
5		7				8		9
	4		2					
	7			9	6			
		4				6		5
	6				4			3

9	5							
4		7			1			
						8	9	7
8	3		4					
	6		3		2		5	
					8		2	4
7	1	6						
			6			2		1
							8	9

	1	4	2					
						6	1	3
			3				5	
	2		6	9				
7	6						8	1
				8	7		4	
	7				4			
1	9	2						
					5	3	7	

	2	1	7	6				
		6		5				1
4	3							7
		7						3
				8				
6						5		
2							6	9
9				2		1		
				1	3	8	7	

2 5 1

				6			2	4
7		6	8					
	5							7
	7		4					8
1	3						4	6
8					7		3	
4							8	
					8	1		5
3	9			5				

2 5 2

		2		4				8
		3	9			5		
4		8		5				
9			3					
	1			2			4	
					7			5
				8		2		7
		4			2	6		
5				1		4		

Puzzle 253:

							2	6
	3	6					7	
5		7		3			4	
4					1			
	6			7			3	
			2					4
	2			5		1		3
	7					9	6	
3	8							

Puzzle 254:

	6				5			9
	9						5	
	8		2	1				
				7			6	8
	2			8			1	
4	1			3				
				5	3		4	
	5						8	
2			6					3

255

		6				2		
		3	2				9	1
						3		
1				4				3
7	6			1			2	4
9				5				7
		8						
4	7				5	8		
		9				5		

256

	3							
			3	1		4		
5	2	7			4	6		
8							5	
7				8				3
	9							8
		3	1			8	9	7
		1		7	6			
							2	

			2					
				9			3	5
		1			8	2	7	
			2	7	8			
3	4						6	2
		8	6	1				
	5	3	7			4		
7	6			8				
					1			

		4	9					5
				6			1	
	9			5			4	
						1	9	
	1		5	7	9		2	
	3	9						
	5			1			6	
	7			9				
2					6	4		

4	3		9				7	
		9			8			
				3	7			5
		7		2				8
				6				
9				5		3		
5			1	7				
			6			2		
	9				5		4	6

4				9				7
1			5			3		
			3	8				6
5						7		
		2		4		8		
		4						9
6				2	3			
		9			1			4
2				7				1

3		9	2			1		
				7		2		3
5		8		9				
		2						
		5	9		7	6		
						8		
				3		9		1
6		3		4				
		1			2	5		4

		9						8
2				4		6		
				8		1	3	
		3			8	9	2	1
9	7	1	6			3		
	4	2		7				
		8		9				2
5						4		

								1
	3		8			5		
4	2			6	9	3		
	8					7		
		5	6		4	8		
		9					2	
		7	1	5			4	6
		2			8		7	
5								

	1			3			2	8
6					9			
9		5			7			
		9			6			5
4								9
1			5			7		
			1			8		3
			3					2
3	8			7			4	

		4	8	3	2			7
3	5			4			2	
		1						
			1					
	3	7				1	6	
					5			
						3		
	1			2			8	9
6			5	9	3	4		

						2	9	5
	6		3				8	
				5		7		
	3	7			6			
9	4						2	8
			1			6	7	
		2		3				
	8				1		4	
4	9	3						

	3				6			
7	4				2	1		
9				7				6
	9			5				4
	7						3	
5				3			1	
6				9				8
		3	8				5	2
			2				7	

	2			9	1		3	
		7						6
		5				4		
			5			3	9	
	7			6			5	
	8	4			2			
		8				1		
6						8		
	9		3	1			4	

		5			9		6	
7	1			3				
6	3		4	7				9
								5
	9						3	
1								
3				9	1		5	4
				4			1	8
	6		7			2		

4			2			1		8
	1				7	3		
	2				6			
				1	3	2		
5								4
		2	9	5				
			8				7	
		4	7				9	
8		7			5			6

2
7
1

		6					9	
		8	5	7	1	4		
					2		5	
	3							2
			7	4	3			
9							4	
	7		1					
		1	6	9	4	8		
	5					6		

2
7
2

9		2					1	7
					6	2		
			8			4	9	6
						1	4	
			2		8			
	4	3						
2	5	9			3			
		8	1					
6	1					9		4

			3			4		
6	3			5	1	8		
	5							
		1			6			4
		2	9		8	7		
5			4			6		
							8	
		5	2	6			3	9
		3			7			

					3	9	6	
								5
6				9	4	1		
			4				3	2
8		4				6		7
7	5				8			
		8	3	4				9
1								
	7	6	5					

275

	1		2	7				3
								6
			9			4		8
8			7			5		
	7			2			9	
		4			9			7
1		8			3			
3								
5				4	2		1	

276

4			7					5
				9	1		3	6
		6				2	9	
						3		1
	7						8	
9		4						
	9	7				5		
8	4		5	6				
5					8			7

	7	5			6			
						4		
		1	9	5	2			
1		9	3		5			7
3			6		4	2		1
			4	6	3	1		
		8						
			1			9	6	

1		3						
5				3	7			9
4				9	2			
	8							
	7		8	5	6		4	
							6	
			4	6				5
3			2	8				4
						9		6

279

	7		4		5	8		
		9		2				3
5					7			4
	2	3						9
1						5	2	
8			3					7
6				1		2		
		1	7		4		8	

280

9	2	8						
		4	7				6	9
			3			5		
		3	2				7	8
7	1				5	9		
		6			8			
1	9				4	6		
						1	2	4

144

7								9
						4		5
8	2				1			
		1		2	6			3
		7		4		8		
3			5	1		9		
			4				5	7
5		3						
9								1

9		8	3				2	
			4					
				2		5	3	
		3	9			7		
	5						6	
		7			5	9		
	2	1		3				
					7			
	8				6	4		1

283

		4		6		1		
8	7			9				
		1	7		3			
		8	4	5				
9								8
			1	6	3			
			6		1	2		
				7			1	3
		6		2		8		

284

		4	2				5	
		6				4	7	
		7			5			2
		3		2				
7				3				9
				9		8		
1			8			6		
	2	9				7		
	6				7	5		

Puzzle 285:

5								1
			6	9				
4	7			8		9		
8								4
	3		6	9	4		2	
2								7
		4		5			8	3
			4	1				
1								5

Puzzle 286:

9		7		6		4	1	
	5			4				
8					7			3
	7	3						
			8		6			
						6	4	
5			7					6
				2			9	
	3	1		5		8		2

5			2		3	4	7	
				4				
2							3	
		2	7				8	
	8			1			4	
	6				5	1		
	9							2
			3					
	7	4	9		8			3

							7	1
9				2	3			
7		5	6		8	3		
							1	5
			1		4			
6	7							
		2	5		1	9		8
			4	8				2
5	4							

		1			2			
			6	7	1			
	7	8			9		4	
		2						3
4	9						5	6
5						8		
	5		8			1	6	
			2	3	4			
			5			4		

							8	3
6		1	8	2		4		
3					6	7		
4					7			
				1				
			5					8
		4	9					1
		2		7	8	9		5
8	6							

291

	9				2			3
8	2	4					9	
		7	1	5				
3						8	2	
	8	9						4
			2	3		1		
	5					4	7	6
1			4				3	

292

8			6	1			7	
7								8
	4		2				3	
1					2	3	6	
	6	4	8					5
	5				6		8	
2								7
	9			2	7			4

		6		4	8			
	2		5					
	3					1	6	
		2	1					
5	6			2			9	1
					5	7		
	1	4					2	
					6		4	
			7	9		8		

				4	6	5		
9							8	
	8				5		1	
		4	2	3				
		3				1		
				1	4	9		
	1		5				2	
	7							8
		9	7	2				

2
9
5

						7		3
				5	4	2		8
			8	7			1	
			3				9	
		9	7		1	6		
	8				2			
	6			2	5			
9		3	4	1				
8		4						

2
9
6

7			2					
				4				3
8	1					6		
	4		6	2		8	3	
		5				2		
	6	3		5	9		4	
		6					2	1
4				7				
					6			9

5								7
				6				8
			9	8		2	1	
3		9	8				4	
	7						2	
	1				4	6		3
	8	4		1	9			
9				3				
7								5

				5		2		9
1	5	8	6					7
	3							
			8	6		9		1
4		6		9	2			
							1	
8					6	7	4	5
7		2		3				

Puzzle 299

7					8			
3	4			6		7		1
	8				4			
		3	4				1	9
1	5				7	8		
			9				5	
5		8		3			2	6
			2					3

Puzzle 300

3			5			6		9
							3	5
	4			8				
2	1		9		6		5	
	9		7		3		8	2
				1			9	
1	3							
9		2			8			7

1

6	9	5	3	8	1	7	4	2
7	8	4	2	5	6	9	1	3
3	1	2	4	9	7	5	6	8
8	6	9	1	4	3	2	7	5
4	5	3	7	2	9	6	8	1
2	7	1	5	6	8	4	3	9
9	4	8	6	1	2	3	5	7
1	3	6	9	7	5	8	2	4
5	2	7	8	3	4	1	9	6

2

6	3	2	9	4	7	8	1	5
5	4	7	1	3	8	6	9	2
9	1	8	6	2	5	7	3	4
4	5	1	2	8	6	3	7	9
2	6	9	3	7	4	5	8	1
8	7	3	5	9	1	2	4	6
3	8	5	4	6	9	1	2	7
1	2	4	7	5	3	9	6	8
7	9	6	8	1	2	4	5	3

3

5	7	3	9	8	1	6	2	4
8	2	1	4	6	3	5	7	9
6	4	9	5	2	7	8	3	1
3	5	8	1	7	9	2	4	6
9	6	7	2	5	4	1	8	3
2	1	4	8	3	6	9	5	7
4	8	6	3	9	2	7	1	5
7	3	2	6	1	5	4	9	8
1	9	5	7	4	8	3	6	2

4

8	4	9	6	7	5	1	3	2
5	6	1	3	2	4	8	7	9
7	3	2	1	9	8	6	4	5
3	1	8	2	5	6	7	9	4
6	2	7	4	3	9	5	1	8
9	5	4	7	8	1	3	2	6
1	8	3	5	4	2	9	6	7
4	9	6	8	1	7	2	5	3
2	7	5	9	6	3	4	8	1

5

2	1	3	5	8	9	4	7	6
8	9	7	2	6	4	5	1	3
4	5	6	7	1	3	8	2	9
6	8	1	4	5	7	3	9	2
3	4	5	9	2	1	7	6	8
7	2	9	8	3	6	1	5	4
1	6	4	3	9	5	2	8	7
9	3	2	1	7	8	6	4	5
5	7	8	6	4	2	9	3	1

6

5	4	3	1	6	9	2	8	7
7	9	8	3	4	2	1	6	5
6	1	2	8	7	5	9	3	4
2	8	4	7	1	3	6	5	9
3	7	1	9	5	6	4	2	8
9	5	6	2	8	4	7	1	3
4	3	5	6	2	7	8	9	1
8	2	7	5	9	1	3	4	6
1	6	9	4	3	8	5	7	2

7

5	9	8	7	2	6	4	1	3
3	6	4	1	5	9	7	2	8
2	7	1	4	3	8	9	6	5
8	3	9	5	1	7	6	4	2
1	4	5	9	6	2	8	3	7
6	2	7	3	8	4	5	9	1
4	5	2	8	9	1	3	7	6
9	1	3	6	7	5	2	8	4
7	8	6	2	4	3	1	5	9

8

2	9	1	8	3	7	6	5	4
7	6	8	5	4	9	2	3	1
3	4	5	2	6	1	8	9	7
4	1	2	6	9	8	5	7	3
5	3	9	7	2	4	1	6	8
6	8	7	1	5	3	4	2	9
1	7	6	9	8	2	3	4	5
9	5	3	4	1	6	7	8	2
8	2	4	3	7	5	9	1	6

9

7	2	9	8	4	1	3	6	5
8	3	4	6	7	5	9	2	1
1	5	6	2	3	9	8	4	7
3	6	7	5	1	8	2	9	4
9	8	5	3	2	4	7	1	6
4	1	2	7	9	6	5	3	8
5	4	3	1	8	2	6	7	9
6	7	1	9	5	3	4	8	2
2	9	8	4	6	7	1	5	3

10

7	2	3	4	6	1	8	9	5
6	4	5	7	9	8	2	1	3
8	1	9	2	3	5	6	7	4
3	8	4	5	1	2	9	6	7
5	7	2	6	8	9	3	4	1
1	9	6	3	7	4	5	8	2
9	6	7	1	5	3	4	2	8
4	3	1	8	2	6	7	5	9
2	5	8	9	4	7	1	3	6

11

6	9	7	8	5	1	2	3	4
2	1	5	4	3	9	6	7	8
8	3	4	7	2	6	5	9	1
1	4	9	2	6	8	3	5	7
5	6	8	3	4	7	9	1	2
7	2	3	1	9	5	8	4	6
3	8	2	9	1	4	7	6	5
4	7	6	5	8	3	1	2	9
9	5	1	6	7	2	4	8	3

12

5	8	2	6	7	1	3	4	9
7	4	1	3	5	9	8	6	2
6	9	3	2	4	8	1	5	7
4	3	5	8	1	7	2	9	6
2	7	9	4	6	3	5	8	1
8	1	6	9	2	5	4	7	3
3	2	4	7	8	6	9	1	5
9	5	7	1	3	4	6	2	8
1	6	8	5	9	2	7	3	4

13

9	7	1	3	2	6	4	5	8
6	3	8	7	4	5	1	2	9
4	2	5	9	8	1	6	7	3
2	8	7	1	9	4	3	6	5
1	9	3	6	5	7	2	8	4
5	4	6	2	3	8	7	9	1
7	5	9	4	1	2	8	3	6
8	1	2	5	6	3	9	4	7
3	6	4	8	7	9	5	1	2

14

3	4	8	2	6	9	1	5	7
6	9	5	1	7	4	2	3	8
1	2	7	8	3	5	9	4	6
9	1	3	6	8	2	5	7	4
2	7	6	5	4	3	8	1	9
8	5	4	9	1	7	6	2	3
7	6	2	3	9	1	4	8	5
4	8	1	7	5	6	3	9	2
5	3	9	4	2	8	7	6	1

15

8	4	9	7	3	5	2	1	6
5	3	1	2	9	6	7	8	4
7	6	2	1	8	4	9	5	3
1	7	6	8	5	9	3	4	2
2	5	3	4	1	7	8	6	9
9	8	4	3	6	2	5	7	1
6	2	7	9	4	8	1	3	5
4	1	8	5	2	3	6	9	7
3	9	5	6	7	1	4	2	8

16

7	9	1	5	3	2	6	8	4
4	3	8	9	6	7	2	1	5
2	6	5	1	4	8	3	7	9
5	4	2	6	7	3	1	9	8
6	8	7	2	1	9	5	4	3
9	1	3	8	5	4	7	2	6
3	5	9	4	2	1	8	6	7
8	2	6	7	9	5	4	3	1
1	7	4	3	8	6	9	5	2

17

3	4	7	2	8	9	5	6	1
9	8	1	7	6	5	3	2	4
2	6	5	1	3	4	7	9	8
5	7	3	9	4	8	2	1	6
4	2	6	3	1	7	8	5	9
1	9	8	6	5	2	4	7	3
6	3	4	5	7	1	9	8	2
8	5	9	4	2	6	1	3	7
7	1	2	8	9	3	6	4	5

18

4	2	7	3	6	9	5	1	8
9	8	6	4	5	1	3	2	7
1	5	3	8	7	2	4	6	9
3	6	2	5	1	7	8	9	4
7	9	4	2	3	8	1	5	6
5	1	8	6	9	4	7	3	2
2	3	9	7	4	5	6	8	1
6	4	1	9	8	3	2	7	5
8	7	5	1	2	6	9	4	3

19

1	9	5	2	7	4	6	3	8
2	7	4	3	6	8	5	1	9
8	3	6	9	5	1	2	7	4
4	8	7	6	2	3	1	9	5
9	2	1	5	4	7	3	8	6
5	6	3	1	8	9	4	2	7
7	5	2	8	1	6	9	4	3
6	4	9	7	3	2	8	5	1
3	1	8	4	9	5	7	6	2

20

6	9	7	1	5	4	8	3	2
4	8	5	3	9	2	7	1	6
1	2	3	6	8	7	9	4	5
7	3	2	8	6	5	1	9	4
9	6	4	2	7	1	3	5	8
8	5	1	4	3	9	2	6	7
2	4	9	7	1	6	5	8	3
3	1	6	5	2	8	4	7	9
5	7	8	9	4	3	6	2	1

21

4	2	9	7	5	1	8	6	3
7	1	5	6	3	8	9	4	2
8	3	6	9	2	4	7	1	5
1	5	8	2	4	6	3	9	7
6	4	2	3	9	7	1	5	8
9	7	3	8	1	5	4	2	6
2	8	7	1	6	9	5	3	4
5	6	1	4	8	3	2	7	9
3	9	4	5	7	2	6	8	1

22

8	4	3	1	5	2	7	6	9
2	5	7	9	4	6	8	1	3
1	6	9	8	3	7	4	5	2
7	1	4	3	2	5	9	8	6
9	2	5	6	8	4	1	3	7
6	3	8	7	9	1	2	4	5
3	7	1	4	6	9	5	2	8
4	8	2	5	7	3	6	9	1
5	9	6	2	1	8	3	7	4

23

9	2	7	3	1	6	5	8	4
8	3	4	9	5	2	6	7	1
5	1	6	8	4	7	3	2	9
2	6	9	1	7	4	8	3	5
7	5	1	2	8	3	9	4	6
4	8	3	5	6	9	2	1	7
3	4	8	6	9	1	7	5	2
6	7	5	4	2	8	1	9	3
1	9	2	7	3	5	4	6	8

24

6	2	5	9	1	4	8	7	3
4	7	9	8	5	3	6	1	2
1	8	3	2	6	7	4	5	9
2	1	6	3	8	9	5	4	7
3	9	8	7	4	5	2	6	1
5	4	7	6	2	1	3	9	8
7	3	4	5	9	2	1	8	6
9	6	1	4	3	8	7	2	5
8	5	2	1	7	6	9	3	4

2/5

2	8	1	5	9	7	4	3	6
5	6	3	2	4	8	7	1	9
4	9	7	1	6	3	2	5	8
7	4	9	6	2	5	1	8	3
1	5	8	9	3	4	6	7	2
6	3	2	8	7	1	9	4	5
9	1	5	4	8	2	3	6	7
3	2	4	7	5	6	8	9	1
8	7	6	3	1	9	5	2	4

2/6

5	6	7	9	4	1	2	8	3
2	1	3	8	6	5	7	9	4
4	9	8	2	7	3	5	1	6
1	2	4	3	8	7	6	5	9
7	3	5	6	1	9	4	2	8
9	8	6	5	2	4	1	3	7
3	7	2	4	5	8	9	6	1
6	4	9	1	3	2	8	7	5
8	5	1	7	9	6	3	4	2

2/7

6	9	4	3	2	5	7	8	1
1	8	7	4	6	9	3	5	2
2	3	5	8	7	1	9	4	6
4	2	3	5	8	7	1	6	9
8	1	9	6	3	2	4	7	5
7	5	6	9	1	4	8	2	3
5	6	8	7	9	3	2	1	4
9	7	1	2	4	6	5	3	8
3	4	2	1	5	8	6	9	7

2/8

3	9	6	7	5	4	8	1	2
8	4	2	6	3	1	9	7	5
5	1	7	8	2	9	3	6	4
7	8	1	9	4	5	2	3	6
4	2	3	1	6	8	7	5	9
6	5	9	3	7	2	1	4	8
1	6	8	5	9	7	4	2	3
2	7	5	4	8	3	6	9	1
9	3	4	2	1	6	5	8	7

2/9

4	9	3	6	5	2	8	7	1
6	5	8	9	7	1	3	4	2
1	2	7	8	4	3	6	5	9
8	1	5	3	2	9	7	6	4
9	6	2	4	8	7	1	3	5
7	3	4	1	6	5	2	9	8
3	8	1	5	9	6	4	2	7
2	4	9	7	3	8	5	1	6
5	7	6	2	1	4	9	8	3

3/0

2	6	3	8	5	4	9	7	1
5	7	8	3	1	9	4	2	6
9	4	1	7	6	2	3	5	8
4	5	6	2	8	7	1	3	9
8	9	2	1	3	6	5	4	7
1	3	7	4	9	5	6	8	2
7	1	4	6	2	3	8	9	5
6	2	5	9	4	8	7	1	3
3	8	9	5	7	1	2	6	4

3/1

2	9	4	5	1	7	3	8	6
8	5	7	3	2	6	9	1	4
6	3	1	9	4	8	2	7	5
4	2	8	1	9	5	6	3	7
9	7	6	8	3	2	4	5	1
5	1	3	6	7	4	8	9	2
3	4	5	2	8	1	7	6	9
1	8	2	7	6	9	5	4	3
7	6	9	4	5	3	1	2	8

3/2

1	8	3	5	2	4	7	6	9
5	4	2	9	6	7	1	3	8
9	7	6	1	3	8	4	2	5
3	1	4	2	7	5	8	9	6
7	9	5	3	8	6	2	4	1
6	2	8	4	9	1	3	5	7
8	3	9	7	5	2	6	1	4
2	6	1	8	4	9	5	7	3
4	5	7	6	1	3	9	8	2

33

4	9	6	3	2	8	5	1	7
5	8	1	9	6	7	2	4	3
7	3	2	4	5	1	6	9	8
6	2	7	8	1	4	9	3	5
3	5	4	6	7	9	8	2	1
9	1	8	2	3	5	4	7	6
2	4	3	1	8	6	7	5	9
8	7	9	5	4	3	1	6	2
1	6	5	7	9	2	3	8	4

34

1	2	4	8	9	6	3	5	7
8	9	7	1	3	5	6	2	4
3	6	5	2	4	7	9	1	8
2	5	3	4	7	1	8	6	9
4	1	6	5	8	9	7	3	2
7	8	9	6	2	3	1	4	5
6	7	2	9	1	4	5	8	3
9	4	1	3	5	8	2	7	6
5	3	8	7	6	2	4	9	1

35

9	1	3	4	7	8	2	6	5
5	8	7	6	2	3	4	9	1
6	2	4	5	9	1	3	8	7
8	7	2	3	4	5	9	1	6
4	5	6	9	1	2	8	7	3
3	9	1	7	8	6	5	2	4
2	4	8	1	5	7	6	3	9
1	6	5	8	3	9	7	4	2
7	3	9	2	6	4	1	5	8

36

9	7	8	1	5	4	6	3	2
6	4	2	7	9	3	5	1	8
5	3	1	6	2	8	4	7	9
3	2	4	5	8	7	1	9	6
8	5	9	4	6	1	7	2	3
1	6	7	9	3	2	8	5	4
2	1	5	3	4	6	9	8	7
4	9	3	8	7	5	2	6	1
7	8	6	2	1	9	3	4	5

37

3	9	8	4	6	7	1	5	2
4	5	1	3	2	8	6	9	7
6	2	7	9	5	1	8	4	3
9	1	4	2	7	3	5	6	8
8	3	5	6	1	9	2	7	4
7	6	2	5	8	4	3	1	9
1	8	6	7	4	2	9	3	5
2	4	9	1	3	5	7	8	6
5	7	3	8	9	6	4	2	1

38

7	6	4	1	9	3	5	8	2
5	1	2	7	8	4	6	9	3
9	3	8	6	2	5	1	4	7
3	5	9	4	7	1	8	2	6
4	2	1	8	3	6	7	5	9
6	8	7	9	5	2	4	3	1
1	9	5	3	6	8	2	7	4
8	4	3	2	1	7	9	6	5
2	7	6	5	4	9	3	1	8

39

4	3	5	9	2	1	6	8	7
7	2	6	5	4	8	3	1	9
1	8	9	7	6	3	5	2	4
5	6	7	4	9	2	1	3	8
2	9	3	8	1	7	4	5	6
8	4	1	3	5	6	9	7	2
6	1	4	2	7	5	8	9	3
3	5	2	6	8	9	7	4	1
9	7	8	1	3	4	2	6	5

40

6	3	2	4	5	8	1	9	7
9	4	8	6	1	7	5	3	2
1	7	5	3	9	2	6	4	8
3	8	1	7	6	9	2	5	4
5	2	6	8	3	4	7	1	9
7	9	4	5	2	1	3	8	6
4	5	7	1	8	6	9	2	3
2	6	3	9	4	5	8	7	1
8	1	9	2	7	3	4	6	5

4/1

1	5	7	2	3	9	4	6	8
8	9	4	7	1	6	3	2	5
6	2	3	5	4	8	9	7	1
7	4	2	8	9	3	5	1	6
5	1	9	6	7	2	8	4	3
3	6	8	4	5	1	2	9	7
4	3	5	9	6	7	1	8	2
2	7	1	3	8	4	6	5	9
9	8	6	1	2	5	7	3	4

4/2

3	5	1	9	4	2	6	8	7
4	2	7	5	8	6	1	3	9
9	8	6	3	7	1	2	4	5
7	6	9	4	2	3	5	1	8
2	3	5	1	9	8	7	6	4
8	1	4	7	6	5	3	9	2
5	4	2	6	3	9	8	7	1
6	7	8	2	1	4	9	5	3
1	9	3	8	5	7	4	2	6

4/3

7	2	4	1	8	6	9	5	3
6	3	5	4	9	7	1	8	2
1	8	9	2	5	3	4	7	6
9	5	7	3	6	8	2	4	1
2	1	8	5	4	9	6	3	7
3	4	6	7	1	2	5	9	8
4	9	3	8	2	1	7	6	5
8	6	2	9	7	5	3	1	4
5	7	1	6	3	4	8	2	9

4/4

6	9	4	2	3	1	8	5	7
3	2	5	8	6	7	4	9	1
1	7	8	5	4	9	3	2	6
5	6	2	9	7	4	1	8	3
9	4	1	3	5	8	6	7	2
8	3	7	1	2	6	5	4	9
2	5	6	4	9	3	7	1	8
7	8	9	6	1	5	2	3	4
4	1	3	7	8	2	9	6	5

4/5

8	7	6	3	5	4	9	1	2
2	3	9	1	6	8	4	7	5
1	5	4	2	9	7	6	8	3
6	2	1	4	7	9	3	5	8
3	9	8	6	1	5	2	4	7
7	4	5	8	2	3	1	9	6
4	6	2	5	8	1	7	3	9
5	1	7	9	3	6	8	2	4
9	8	3	7	4	2	5	6	1

4/6

3	2	4	7	5	1	9	8	6
9	8	1	2	6	4	3	7	5
7	5	6	9	8	3	1	4	2
8	4	5	6	9	2	7	3	1
2	7	9	1	3	8	6	5	4
6	1	3	4	7	5	8	2	9
5	6	2	3	1	7	4	9	8
1	3	8	5	4	9	2	6	7
4	9	7	8	2	6	5	1	3

4/7

4	7	9	1	6	3	2	5	8
6	2	3	8	7	5	1	4	9
1	8	5	4	9	2	6	7	3
7	3	2	6	5	8	4	9	1
5	4	6	3	1	9	7	8	2
9	1	8	2	4	7	5	3	6
2	5	4	9	8	6	3	1	7
8	6	7	5	3	1	9	2	4
3	9	1	7	2	4	8	6	5

4/8

5	4	7	6	2	9	1	8	3
2	8	9	1	3	5	7	4	6
3	1	6	8	7	4	2	5	9
6	2	1	3	5	8	4	9	7
9	5	4	2	1	7	6	3	8
8	7	3	9	4	6	5	1	2
7	6	8	4	9	1	3	2	5
1	3	5	7	8	2	9	6	4
4	9	2	5	6	3	8	7	1

49

4	9	7	1	5	8	6	3	2
8	1	5	3	2	6	4	9	7
6	3	2	7	9	4	1	5	8
3	6	8	4	1	5	2	7	9
9	2	1	6	3	7	5	8	4
5	7	4	2	8	9	3	1	6
7	4	9	5	6	3	8	2	1
1	5	6	8	7	2	9	4	3
2	8	3	9	4	1	7	6	5

50

1	7	6	9	4	2	5	3	8
2	9	5	3	6	8	4	1	7
4	8	3	7	5	1	9	2	6
6	2	9	4	1	7	3	8	5
3	5	4	8	2	6	1	7	9
7	1	8	5	9	3	6	4	2
5	3	1	2	7	9	8	6	4
9	6	2	1	8	4	7	5	3
8	4	7	6	3	5	2	9	1

51

1	9	8	6	7	5	4	3	2
3	4	7	2	8	9	5	1	6
5	6	2	4	1	3	7	9	8
7	5	3	9	6	1	8	2	4
9	2	6	8	3	4	1	7	5
8	1	4	7	5	2	3	6	9
6	7	5	1	2	8	9	4	3
2	3	9	5	4	7	6	8	1
4	8	1	3	9	6	2	5	7

52

5	1	7	6	3	9	2	4	8
8	2	3	7	1	4	9	6	5
6	9	4	5	8	2	3	1	7
9	8	6	1	2	7	4	5	3
3	7	1	9	4	5	8	2	6
2	4	5	8	6	3	7	9	1
1	6	2	3	9	8	5	7	4
4	5	8	2	7	6	1	3	9
7	3	9	4	5	1	6	8	2

53

6	4	9	2	5	8	3	1	7
1	5	8	7	3	6	2	4	9
3	2	7	1	4	9	6	8	5
2	1	3	4	8	5	9	7	6
9	6	4	3	2	7	8	5	1
7	8	5	9	6	1	4	3	2
8	7	2	6	1	3	5	9	4
5	9	6	8	7	4	1	2	3
4	3	1	5	9	2	7	6	8

54

4	8	9	1	5	3	7	2	6
6	3	2	7	9	4	1	8	5
1	7	5	2	8	6	4	3	9
3	9	1	8	4	5	6	7	2
8	2	4	6	7	1	5	9	3
5	6	7	3	2	9	8	4	1
2	4	6	9	1	8	3	5	7
9	1	8	5	3	7	2	6	4
7	5	3	4	6	2	9	1	8

55

5	6	4	8	3	7	1	2	9
7	9	1	2	5	4	3	8	6
2	8	3	9	6	1	4	5	7
6	2	5	7	8	3	9	4	1
9	4	7	1	2	5	8	6	3
3	1	8	4	9	6	2	7	5
8	5	6	3	1	2	7	9	4
1	7	9	5	4	8	6	3	2
4	3	2	6	7	9	5	1	8

56

4	6	1	8	5	9	2	7	3
5	9	8	3	7	2	4	6	1
7	3	2	1	6	4	9	5	8
9	4	3	6	2	7	8	1	5
1	7	5	9	8	3	6	2	4
2	8	6	5	4	1	3	9	7
8	2	9	7	3	5	1	4	6
3	5	4	2	1	6	7	8	9
6	1	7	4	9	8	5	3	2

57

3	8	7	9	5	6	1	4	2
9	6	1	8	2	4	3	5	7
4	2	5	7	1	3	8	9	6
6	5	8	3	4	9	2	7	1
7	4	2	1	8	5	6	3	9
1	3	9	6	7	2	4	8	5
8	1	6	5	3	7	9	2	4
2	7	3	4	9	1	5	6	8
5	9	4	2	6	8	7	1	3

58

9	1	3	7	6	2	5	8	4
8	2	7	9	5	4	3	1	6
4	5	6	8	3	1	9	7	2
3	8	9	4	2	6	1	5	7
5	4	2	1	7	9	8	6	3
6	7	1	3	8	5	4	2	9
1	3	5	2	9	7	6	4	8
2	6	8	5	4	3	7	9	1
7	9	4	6	1	8	2	3	5

59

4	7	3	1	5	9	2	8	6
1	2	8	6	4	3	9	5	7
6	9	5	2	7	8	1	3	4
7	8	4	9	3	1	5	6	2
3	6	1	7	2	5	8	4	9
9	5	2	4	8	6	7	1	3
2	3	6	5	1	7	4	9	8
5	4	9	8	6	2	3	7	1
8	1	7	3	9	4	6	2	5

60

1	2	7	4	5	3	9	6	8
5	8	3	7	9	6	4	2	1
4	6	9	1	8	2	5	3	7
9	4	2	8	3	5	7	1	6
3	7	5	9	6	1	2	8	4
6	1	8	2	4	7	3	9	5
2	3	6	5	1	4	8	7	9
8	5	1	3	7	9	6	4	2
7	9	4	6	2	8	1	5	3

61

8	7	1	2	5	3	9	4	6
4	5	6	7	1	9	8	2	3
2	3	9	4	6	8	1	5	7
5	1	2	6	8	4	7	3	9
9	6	3	5	7	1	4	8	2
7	4	8	9	3	2	6	1	5
1	9	7	8	2	5	3	6	4
6	8	5	3	4	7	2	9	1
3	2	4	1	9	6	5	7	8

62

9	8	6	3	7	5	2	1	4
2	3	4	8	1	9	5	7	6
7	5	1	6	2	4	3	9	8
1	6	3	2	9	8	4	5	7
5	7	9	4	3	6	1	8	2
4	2	8	7	5	1	9	6	3
8	4	5	1	6	3	7	2	9
6	1	2	9	4	7	8	3	5
3	9	7	5	8	2	6	4	1

63

9	4	2	6	8	3	5	7	1
7	5	3	1	2	9	6	4	8
8	1	6	7	5	4	3	2	9
2	7	9	8	3	1	4	6	5
5	8	4	2	7	6	1	9	3
6	3	1	9	4	5	7	8	2
4	2	5	3	9	7	8	1	6
1	9	7	5	6	8	2	3	4
3	6	8	4	1	2	9	5	7

64

1	7	6	4	8	9	5	2	3
3	8	9	2	5	6	7	1	4
2	5	4	3	7	1	9	8	6
5	9	2	1	3	7	6	4	8
6	3	1	9	4	8	2	5	7
8	4	7	6	2	5	1	3	9
4	6	5	8	9	2	3	7	1
9	2	3	7	1	4	8	6	5
7	1	8	5	6	3	4	9	2

65

4	2	6	9	3	8	5	7	1
3	1	7	4	5	6	8	2	9
8	9	5	2	1	7	3	4	6
1	5	8	6	9	2	4	3	7
2	6	4	5	7	3	9	1	8
9	7	3	1	8	4	2	6	5
5	8	2	7	4	1	6	9	3
6	3	1	8	2	9	7	5	4
7	4	9	3	6	5	1	8	2

66

1	4	5	8	9	7	6	2	3
8	6	7	5	3	2	1	9	4
2	9	3	1	6	4	8	7	5
7	2	4	3	1	6	9	5	8
3	8	1	7	5	9	4	6	2
6	5	9	2	4	8	7	3	1
5	1	8	6	7	3	2	4	9
9	7	2	4	8	5	3	1	6
4	3	6	9	2	1	5	8	7

67

3	6	8	5	4	7	1	9	2
9	4	5	1	2	8	3	6	7
7	2	1	9	6	3	5	8	4
1	7	4	6	3	2	9	5	8
8	3	9	7	5	4	6	2	1
6	5	2	8	9	1	4	7	3
4	9	7	3	8	6	2	1	5
2	8	6	4	1	5	7	3	9
5	1	3	2	7	9	8	4	6

68

3	9	7	8	1	4	6	5	2
2	8	5	9	6	3	1	7	4
6	4	1	7	5	2	9	3	8
8	1	4	5	3	6	7	2	9
9	6	3	2	7	8	5	4	1
7	5	2	4	9	1	3	8	6
5	2	6	1	4	7	8	9	3
4	3	9	6	8	5	2	1	7
1	7	8	3	2	9	4	6	5

69

7	1	5	4	3	6	8	9	2
8	3	2	1	5	9	4	6	7
6	4	9	7	2	8	1	5	3
2	5	8	9	1	4	3	7	6
4	6	7	3	8	2	5	1	9
3	9	1	6	7	5	2	4	8
1	8	3	5	6	7	9	2	4
5	7	4	2	9	3	6	8	1
9	2	6	8	4	1	7	3	5

70

4	7	1	8	6	3	2	9	5
2	5	6	1	7	9	8	4	3
8	3	9	4	5	2	6	7	1
6	2	8	3	4	1	7	5	9
9	4	3	5	2	7	1	6	8
5	1	7	9	8	6	3	2	4
1	9	2	6	3	4	5	8	7
3	6	5	7	9	8	4	1	2
7	8	4	2	1	5	9	3	6

71

1	3	2	7	6	8	4	9	5
9	5	6	1	4	2	3	8	7
7	4	8	9	3	5	6	1	2
8	9	4	3	5	6	7	2	1
5	6	3	2	1	7	9	4	8
2	1	7	8	9	4	5	6	3
6	2	1	4	7	3	8	5	9
4	7	9	5	8	1	2	3	6
3	8	5	6	2	9	1	7	4

72

2	5	8	7	6	1	9	4	3
7	6	1	4	3	9	2	5	8
9	4	3	2	8	5	7	1	6
1	3	2	9	4	8	6	7	5
6	9	5	1	7	3	4	8	2
4	8	7	5	2	6	3	9	1
5	7	6	3	1	4	8	2	9
3	2	9	8	5	7	1	6	4
8	1	4	6	9	2	5	3	7

73

7	1	4	8	9	2	3	6	5
6	9	3	7	1	5	4	8	2
5	2	8	4	3	6	7	1	9
1	8	7	9	5	3	2	4	6
9	5	2	6	7	4	8	3	1
4	3	6	2	8	1	9	5	7
8	7	5	1	4	9	6	2	3
2	4	1	3	6	7	5	9	8
3	6	9	5	2	8	1	7	4

74

1	9	5	7	4	3	8	6	2
4	2	7	6	9	8	1	5	3
3	6	8	1	5	2	9	7	4
9	4	2	8	3	5	7	1	6
8	7	6	4	2	1	3	9	5
5	3	1	9	7	6	2	4	8
2	1	4	5	8	7	6	3	9
6	8	9	3	1	4	5	2	7
7	5	3	2	6	9	4	8	1

75

4	7	2	6	9	5	1	3	8
6	3	9	7	8	1	4	5	2
5	8	1	4	2	3	6	7	9
1	4	3	5	6	2	9	8	7
2	9	7	8	1	4	3	6	5
8	6	5	9	3	7	2	1	4
3	2	4	1	7	8	5	9	6
9	5	8	3	4	6	7	2	1
7	1	6	2	5	9	8	4	3

76

8	3	5	2	4	7	9	6	1
2	1	7	9	5	6	4	8	3
6	4	9	8	3	1	7	5	2
9	5	6	4	1	8	2	3	7
1	8	3	7	2	5	6	4	9
4	7	2	6	9	3	8	1	5
7	2	1	5	6	4	3	9	8
5	9	4	3	8	2	1	7	6
3	6	8	1	7	9	5	2	4

77

8	7	5	1	6	2	3	4	9
4	3	2	7	9	8	5	6	1
9	1	6	5	4	3	8	7	2
3	6	7	4	5	1	2	9	8
2	4	9	8	3	6	7	1	5
5	8	1	2	7	9	4	3	6
6	5	4	9	8	7	1	2	3
7	2	3	6	1	5	9	8	4
1	9	8	3	2	4	6	5	7

78

2	3	6	5	8	4	7	1	9
8	1	7	9	2	6	4	3	5
9	4	5	7	1	3	8	6	2
1	7	4	6	5	2	9	8	3
5	6	2	3	9	8	1	4	7
3	8	9	4	7	1	2	5	6
4	9	3	1	6	7	5	2	8
7	2	1	8	3	5	6	9	4
6	5	8	2	4	9	3	7	1

79

7	3	6	9	5	8	4	1	2
9	4	1	7	6	2	3	5	8
8	5	2	1	4	3	9	6	7
4	9	3	5	1	7	8	2	6
2	1	8	6	3	4	5	7	9
5	6	7	8	2	9	1	4	3
6	8	9	4	7	5	2	3	1
3	7	4	2	9	1	6	8	5
1	2	5	3	8	6	7	9	4

80

2	3	5	8	7	9	6	4	1
6	8	1	2	3	4	5	7	9
7	4	9	6	1	5	8	2	3
4	9	2	1	8	3	7	6	5
8	5	3	7	9	6	2	1	4
1	7	6	5	4	2	9	3	8
5	1	8	4	6	7	3	9	2
3	6	4	9	2	8	1	5	7
9	2	7	3	5	1	4	8	6

8/1

7	3	6	9	2	8	1	4	5
9	4	1	6	5	7	2	8	3
8	2	5	4	3	1	6	7	9
5	9	3	7	4	6	8	1	2
6	1	2	5	8	3	7	9	4
4	8	7	2	1	9	3	5	6
3	6	4	1	7	5	9	2	8
1	5	8	3	9	2	4	6	7
2	7	9	8	6	4	5	3	1

8/2

5	7	9	2	8	1	4	6	3
6	1	8	3	4	9	5	7	2
2	4	3	6	5	7	9	1	8
8	5	1	7	3	4	2	9	6
4	9	7	1	2	6	3	8	5
3	2	6	8	9	5	7	4	1
7	6	4	5	1	3	8	2	9
1	3	2	9	7	8	6	5	4
9	8	5	4	6	2	1	3	7

8/3

5	4	9	3	7	2	1	6	8
2	7	3	1	8	6	5	4	9
6	1	8	9	5	4	2	7	3
7	8	6	2	4	9	3	1	5
9	5	1	6	3	7	8	2	4
4	3	2	8	1	5	6	9	7
1	9	7	5	2	3	4	8	6
8	6	5	4	9	1	7	3	2
3	2	4	7	6	8	9	5	1

8/4

6	9	3	8	1	7	5	2	4
4	1	5	2	3	9	6	8	7
2	7	8	4	6	5	1	9	3
7	8	6	1	4	2	9	3	5
3	4	9	6	5	8	2	7	1
5	2	1	7	9	3	4	6	8
9	3	2	5	7	4	8	1	6
8	6	4	3	2	1	7	5	9
1	5	7	9	8	6	3	4	2

8/5

7	1	3	2	8	6	9	5	4
6	2	8	4	9	5	7	3	1
4	9	5	7	1	3	2	6	8
1	6	2	9	5	4	8	7	3
9	5	7	1	3	8	4	2	6
8	3	4	6	2	7	5	1	9
3	8	1	5	7	9	6	4	2
5	4	9	3	6	2	1	8	7
2	7	6	8	4	1	3	9	5

8/6

4	9	7	6	3	1	5	8	2
5	8	3	4	2	9	6	1	7
1	2	6	7	5	8	9	3	4
7	6	9	8	1	4	2	5	3
2	1	4	5	6	3	8	7	9
3	5	8	2	9	7	1	4	6
6	3	5	1	7	2	4	9	8
8	7	1	9	4	6	3	2	5
9	4	2	3	8	5	7	6	1

8/7

7	5	8	1	9	4	6	3	2
3	4	2	6	7	8	5	1	9
6	1	9	3	2	5	7	8	4
5	6	1	8	4	2	3	9	7
4	2	3	9	6	7	1	5	8
8	9	7	5	3	1	2	4	6
2	3	4	7	5	9	8	6	1
9	8	6	2	1	3	4	7	5
1	7	5	4	8	6	9	2	3

8/8

2	9	7	4	3	1	6	8	5
1	4	8	6	7	5	2	9	3
6	3	5	8	2	9	4	1	7
8	2	9	7	5	6	3	4	1
4	6	3	1	9	8	7	5	2
5	7	1	3	4	2	9	6	8
7	8	2	9	1	4	5	3	6
9	5	6	2	8	3	1	7	4
3	1	4	5	6	7	8	2	9

8/9

5	9	8	3	4	2	6	7	1
6	4	1	7	9	8	3	5	2
2	7	3	1	6	5	9	4	8
3	2	6	4	5	7	1	8	9
4	8	9	2	1	3	7	6	5
1	5	7	9	8	6	2	3	4
7	1	4	5	3	9	8	2	6
9	6	2	8	7	4	5	1	3
8	3	5	6	2	1	4	9	7

9/0

1	9	6	2	4	8	5	7	3
8	4	2	5	3	7	6	9	1
5	3	7	9	1	6	4	2	8
7	6	4	1	2	5	8	3	9
3	1	8	6	9	4	2	5	7
9	2	5	8	7	3	1	6	4
6	5	3	4	8	9	7	1	2
2	8	9	7	6	1	3	4	5
4	7	1	3	5	2	9	8	6

9/1

6	8	2	7	9	5	4	3	1
9	3	4	2	1	8	6	5	7
7	1	5	3	6	4	9	8	2
4	9	6	8	7	1	3	2	5
5	7	3	4	2	9	1	6	8
8	2	1	5	3	6	7	9	4
1	5	9	6	4	2	8	7	3
3	6	8	1	5	7	2	4	9
2	4	7	9	8	3	5	1	6

9/2

6	3	5	7	8	9	1	4	2
1	4	2	3	6	5	8	9	7
8	9	7	2	1	4	6	3	5
5	2	8	1	4	3	7	6	9
9	6	4	8	7	2	5	1	3
7	1	3	5	9	6	4	2	8
3	7	9	6	5	1	2	8	4
2	8	1	4	3	7	9	5	6
4	5	6	9	2	8	3	7	1

9/3

3	1	4	8	2	9	6	5	7
9	7	2	1	5	6	4	3	8
5	6	8	4	7	3	2	1	9
6	8	5	2	9	1	3	7	4
1	3	7	6	8	4	5	9	2
4	2	9	5	3	7	1	8	6
2	4	3	7	1	8	9	6	5
8	5	1	9	6	2	7	4	3
7	9	6	3	4	5	8	2	1

9/4

8	7	1	6	3	2	9	4	5
2	9	5	8	7	4	6	1	3
4	6	3	5	1	9	8	7	2
6	1	4	9	5	7	3	2	8
9	2	7	3	8	6	1	5	4
3	5	8	4	2	1	7	6	9
7	8	9	1	4	5	2	3	6
5	3	2	7	6	8	4	9	1
1	4	6	2	9	3	5	8	7

9/5

5	6	8	3	1	9	2	4	7
1	2	4	8	6	7	3	5	9
9	7	3	4	2	5	6	8	1
3	8	5	6	4	1	9	7	2
6	4	7	2	9	8	1	3	5
2	1	9	7	5	3	8	6	4
8	9	1	5	7	6	4	2	3
4	5	6	9	3	2	7	1	8
7	3	2	1	8	4	5	9	6

9/6

3	1	5	6	9	7	2	4	8
8	7	9	2	4	5	6	1	3
4	6	2	8	1	3	7	9	5
9	5	7	4	6	1	3	8	2
1	8	3	7	5	2	9	6	4
6	2	4	3	8	9	5	7	1
2	4	8	9	3	6	1	5	7
5	3	6	1	7	8	4	2	9
7	9	1	5	2	4	8	3	6

97

8	2	5	3	4	7	9	6	1
9	3	7	1	8	6	2	5	4
6	1	4	9	5	2	7	8	3
4	5	1	8	3	9	6	2	7
3	6	9	2	7	4	8	1	5
2	7	8	6	1	5	4	3	9
7	8	3	4	2	1	5	9	6
1	4	6	5	9	8	3	7	2
5	9	2	7	6	3	1	4	8

98

5	4	6	3	7	2	9	1	8
3	9	1	6	8	4	7	2	5
7	2	8	1	5	9	6	3	4
8	5	4	7	6	1	2	9	3
9	7	2	5	4	3	1	8	6
1	6	3	9	2	8	4	5	7
4	1	5	2	3	7	8	6	9
6	8	9	4	1	5	3	7	2
2	3	7	8	9	6	5	4	1

99

9	6	7	2	5	8	3	4	1
5	2	8	1	4	3	7	9	6
4	1	3	7	6	9	5	8	2
1	5	6	3	8	2	9	7	4
7	3	2	9	1	4	8	6	5
8	9	4	6	7	5	1	2	3
6	8	9	5	2	1	4	3	7
3	7	1	4	9	6	2	5	8
2	4	5	8	3	7	6	1	9

100

6	7	4	1	5	2	9	3	8
8	9	5	7	3	4	1	2	6
3	1	2	9	8	6	5	7	4
1	4	7	2	9	3	6	8	5
2	3	8	5	6	1	7	4	9
9	5	6	4	7	8	2	1	3
5	8	1	3	2	9	4	6	7
4	6	9	8	1	7	3	5	2
7	2	3	6	4	5	8	9	1

101

1	6	9	2	3	4	7	5	8
3	5	8	7	1	9	2	6	4
4	2	7	8	6	5	1	3	9
9	1	5	3	7	2	8	4	6
8	7	4	5	9	6	3	2	1
2	3	6	1	4	8	9	7	5
6	8	2	9	5	7	4	1	3
7	4	1	6	8	3	5	9	2
5	9	3	4	2	1	6	8	7

102

7	9	1	8	6	3	5	4	2
3	4	5	9	2	1	8	7	6
2	6	8	5	4	7	1	3	9
6	7	2	4	1	9	3	8	5
9	5	4	3	7	8	2	6	1
1	8	3	6	5	2	7	9	4
4	2	7	1	3	6	9	5	8
5	1	9	7	8	4	6	2	3
8	3	6	2	9	5	4	1	7

103

9	8	4	6	1	7	5	3	2
1	3	7	9	2	5	6	4	8
5	6	2	8	4	3	9	1	7
4	5	6	2	9	8	3	7	1
3	1	9	5	7	4	2	8	6
2	7	8	1	3	6	4	9	5
7	9	5	4	6	1	8	2	3
6	4	3	7	8	2	1	5	9
8	2	1	3	5	9	7	6	4

104

7	6	8	2	1	9	5	4	3
2	4	3	8	6	5	9	7	1
1	9	5	4	7	3	2	6	8
9	2	6	1	5	7	8	3	4
8	5	4	3	2	6	1	9	7
3	1	7	9	8	4	6	5	2
6	3	1	5	4	2	7	8	9
4	7	2	6	9	8	3	1	5
5	8	9	7	3	1	4	2	6

105

1	2	4	7	9	3	5	6	8
5	6	9	2	1	8	4	3	7
7	8	3	5	4	6	2	9	1
6	5	2	1	8	4	3	7	9
4	9	7	3	6	2	8	1	5
3	1	8	9	5	7	6	2	4
8	3	6	4	7	1	9	5	2
2	7	5	8	3	9	1	4	6
9	4	1	6	2	5	7	8	3

106

8	6	9	1	2	4	3	7	5
4	3	5	6	9	7	2	8	1
7	1	2	5	8	3	6	9	4
3	9	1	8	7	6	5	4	2
2	7	4	9	5	1	8	3	6
6	5	8	4	3	2	9	1	7
9	8	6	7	1	5	4	2	3
1	4	3	2	6	8	7	5	9
5	2	7	3	4	9	1	6	8

107

4	1	7	3	2	8	6	5	9
3	6	8	1	9	5	4	7	2
5	9	2	6	4	7	3	8	1
8	2	3	7	5	6	1	9	4
1	7	5	4	3	9	8	2	6
6	4	9	2	8	1	5	3	7
2	3	6	5	7	4	9	1	8
7	8	4	9	1	3	2	6	5
9	5	1	8	6	2	7	4	3

108

9	3	4	1	7	8	6	5	2
5	8	6	2	4	3	9	7	1
7	1	2	6	9	5	3	8	4
2	4	8	5	6	1	7	3	9
1	9	7	3	8	4	2	6	5
6	5	3	7	2	9	1	4	8
8	6	5	9	3	2	4	1	7
4	7	9	8	1	6	5	2	3
3	2	1	4	5	7	8	9	6

109

7	4	3	1	8	6	5	2	9
9	1	8	3	5	2	4	7	6
5	2	6	9	4	7	3	8	1
2	6	1	8	7	5	9	3	4
4	7	9	6	2	3	1	5	8
8	3	5	4	9	1	7	6	2
3	9	2	7	6	4	8	1	5
1	5	4	2	3	8	6	9	7
6	8	7	5	1	9	2	4	3

110

9	7	5	8	4	6	1	3	2
8	3	6	7	2	1	9	5	4
1	2	4	5	9	3	7	6	8
5	1	9	6	8	4	3	2	7
4	6	3	2	1	7	5	8	9
2	8	7	3	5	9	4	1	6
3	4	1	9	6	8	2	7	5
6	9	2	1	7	5	8	4	3
7	5	8	4	3	2	6	9	1

111

9	8	2	1	5	3	7	4	6
5	3	1	7	6	4	8	9	2
4	6	7	2	8	9	3	1	5
3	5	4	9	1	8	2	6	7
1	2	8	3	7	6	4	5	9
7	9	6	4	2	5	1	8	3
8	7	5	6	4	2	9	3	1
6	1	9	8	3	7	5	2	4
2	4	3	5	9	1	6	7	8

112

4	8	2	5	9	6	3	7	1
6	9	7	8	1	3	4	2	5
5	3	1	7	2	4	6	9	8
7	5	8	4	6	2	1	3	9
1	4	9	3	7	8	2	5	6
3	2	6	9	5	1	7	8	4
2	7	5	1	4	9	8	6	3
8	6	4	2	3	5	9	1	7
9	1	3	6	8	7	5	4	2

113

6	3	7	5	8	9	4	2	1
2	1	4	6	7	3	8	5	9
5	8	9	4	2	1	3	7	6
3	9	1	7	5	6	2	8	4
7	5	2	8	9	4	6	1	3
8	4	6	1	3	2	7	9	5
9	2	8	3	4	5	1	6	7
1	7	3	9	6	8	5	4	2
4	6	5	2	1	7	9	3	8

114

4	8	1	3	9	6	7	2	5
9	3	2	4	5	7	8	6	1
5	7	6	8	1	2	9	3	4
1	9	3	6	2	5	4	7	8
2	5	4	7	8	9	3	1	6
7	6	8	1	4	3	5	9	2
3	1	9	5	6	8	2	4	7
6	2	5	9	7	4	1	8	3
8	4	7	2	3	1	6	5	9

115

8	7	2	6	9	1	3	4	5
4	3	9	2	7	5	1	8	6
1	5	6	4	8	3	7	9	2
6	2	3	5	4	7	8	1	9
9	1	4	8	2	6	5	7	3
5	8	7	1	3	9	2	6	4
7	4	5	9	1	2	6	3	8
3	6	8	7	5	4	9	2	1
2	9	1	3	6	8	4	5	7

116

8	9	1	4	3	7	2	5	6
3	6	5	9	1	2	4	7	8
4	2	7	5	8	6	3	1	9
9	5	8	3	6	1	7	2	4
7	4	2	8	5	9	6	3	1
1	3	6	2	7	4	8	9	5
6	8	9	1	2	3	5	4	7
5	1	3	7	4	8	9	6	2
2	7	4	6	9	5	1	8	3

117

3	7	8	6	2	4	5	1	9
2	6	1	5	9	7	8	3	4
5	4	9	1	8	3	7	6	2
9	1	2	3	7	6	4	8	5
6	8	4	2	5	9	1	7	3
7	5	3	4	1	8	2	9	6
1	2	7	9	6	5	3	4	8
4	9	5	8	3	1	6	2	7
8	3	6	7	4	2	9	5	1

118

9	6	5	1	7	8	2	3	4
7	4	2	9	5	3	6	8	1
8	3	1	4	6	2	7	9	5
6	1	3	8	2	4	5	7	9
2	7	9	5	3	6	1	4	8
4	5	8	7	1	9	3	2	6
5	9	6	3	8	7	4	1	2
1	8	7	2	4	5	9	6	3
3	2	4	6	9	1	8	5	7

119

8	2	4	9	7	5	3	1	6
9	3	7	6	4	1	5	2	8
5	1	6	2	8	3	9	7	4
6	4	9	5	2	8	1	3	7
2	8	5	3	1	7	4	6	9
1	7	3	4	9	6	2	8	5
3	6	2	7	5	9	8	4	1
7	5	8	1	3	4	6	9	2
4	9	1	8	6	2	7	5	3

120

9	1	6	2	4	7	5	3	8
3	4	7	5	8	1	9	6	2
8	5	2	6	3	9	4	7	1
5	3	9	8	6	2	7	1	4
7	6	8	4	1	5	3	2	9
1	2	4	7	9	3	6	8	5
4	7	5	1	2	6	8	9	3
2	8	3	9	7	4	1	5	6
6	9	1	3	5	8	2	4	7

121

1	9	8	3	7	2	4	5	6
5	4	2	1	8	6	7	3	9
6	3	7	4	5	9	1	8	2
3	8	6	7	4	1	9	2	5
9	7	1	6	2	5	8	4	3
2	5	4	8	9	3	6	1	7
4	2	9	5	6	8	3	7	1
7	6	3	2	1	4	5	9	8
8	1	5	9	3	7	2	6	4

122

5	7	1	3	6	9	2	4	8
2	6	8	5	7	4	9	1	3
9	3	4	2	8	1	5	7	6
3	2	9	1	4	6	8	5	7
1	8	7	9	2	5	3	6	4
6	4	5	7	3	8	1	9	2
7	5	2	4	9	3	6	8	1
8	1	3	6	5	7	4	2	9
4	9	6	8	1	2	7	3	5

123

4	5	9	1	3	2	6	8	7
3	2	6	4	7	8	9	5	1
8	1	7	5	9	6	4	3	2
5	8	4	9	1	3	7	2	6
7	9	2	6	8	5	1	4	3
1	6	3	2	4	7	5	9	8
2	4	5	8	6	1	3	7	9
6	7	8	3	5	9	2	1	4
9	3	1	7	2	4	8	6	5

124

9	5	7	2	3	4	1	6	8
8	1	3	9	6	7	2	4	5
4	6	2	1	8	5	9	7	3
2	3	4	8	1	6	5	9	7
1	9	5	7	4	3	6	8	2
6	7	8	5	9	2	4	3	1
3	8	1	4	5	9	7	2	6
5	2	9	6	7	8	3	1	4
7	4	6	3	2	1	8	5	9

125

3	9	8	5	2	7	6	4	1
1	6	5	4	8	3	7	2	9
7	4	2	9	1	6	8	3	5
5	1	7	6	4	9	3	8	2
8	2	4	3	7	1	5	9	6
6	3	9	2	5	8	4	1	7
9	8	6	7	3	2	1	5	4
2	5	3	1	6	4	9	7	8
4	7	1	8	9	5	2	6	3

126

3	1	2	8	7	9	4	5	6
9	4	5	3	2	6	7	8	1
7	8	6	5	4	1	3	2	9
4	5	1	2	6	3	9	7	8
2	9	8	7	1	4	5	6	3
6	3	7	9	8	5	2	1	4
8	2	9	6	3	7	1	4	5
1	6	3	4	5	2	8	9	7
5	7	4	1	9	8	6	3	2

127

8	7	6	4	5	9	2	1	3
4	5	3	1	7	2	8	9	6
2	9	1	6	3	8	4	5	7
7	6	5	8	2	4	9	3	1
1	3	8	9	6	7	5	4	2
9	4	2	5	1	3	7	6	8
6	8	4	7	9	1	3	2	5
5	2	7	3	4	6	1	8	9
3	1	9	2	8	5	6	7	4

128

5	1	6	2	4	7	9	8	3
8	7	2	1	3	9	5	6	4
3	9	4	6	8	5	2	7	1
2	5	7	9	1	8	3	4	6
9	3	8	7	6	4	1	5	2
4	6	1	3	5	2	7	9	8
7	4	3	8	9	1	6	2	5
6	8	9	5	2	3	4	1	7
1	2	5	4	7	6	8	3	9

129

4	3	9	1	5	7	8	2	6
6	8	1	9	3	2	5	7	4
2	5	7	6	4	8	3	1	9
7	9	8	4	1	3	2	6	5
1	2	4	5	8	6	9	3	7
5	6	3	2	7	9	4	8	1
9	4	2	3	6	1	7	5	8
3	7	6	8	9	5	1	4	2
8	1	5	7	2	4	6	9	3

130

9	1	6	5	3	7	8	4	2
2	7	3	8	4	1	9	6	5
8	5	4	6	2	9	1	7	3
5	9	1	3	6	8	4	2	7
4	3	7	1	5	2	6	9	8
6	8	2	7	9	4	5	3	1
1	4	8	9	7	3	2	5	6
3	6	9	2	8	5	7	1	4
7	2	5	4	1	6	3	8	9

131

8	2	7	5	9	4	3	1	6
1	9	4	8	6	3	2	5	7
6	3	5	7	1	2	4	9	8
4	5	1	6	3	7	8	2	9
3	7	8	9	2	1	6	4	5
2	6	9	4	5	8	1	7	3
5	1	3	2	8	9	7	6	4
7	8	6	1	4	5	9	3	2
9	4	2	3	7	6	5	8	1

132

8	2	5	7	9	6	4	3	1
9	4	1	8	3	2	5	6	7
7	3	6	1	4	5	2	9	8
1	8	4	3	6	7	9	2	5
5	7	3	2	1	9	8	4	6
6	9	2	5	8	4	1	7	3
2	5	8	9	7	3	6	1	4
4	1	7	6	2	8	3	5	9
3	6	9	4	5	1	7	8	2

133

7	9	8	1	3	4	6	2	5
2	5	3	9	7	6	8	1	4
6	4	1	5	8	2	7	9	3
9	1	4	8	6	7	3	5	2
5	8	6	3	2	9	4	7	1
3	7	2	4	5	1	9	6	8
8	6	5	7	1	3	2	4	9
1	2	9	6	4	8	5	3	7
4	3	7	2	9	5	1	8	6

134

2	6	3	4	8	1	7	5	9
4	8	1	5	7	9	6	2	3
7	9	5	2	3	6	8	1	4
1	3	2	6	9	5	4	7	8
8	7	9	1	4	3	5	6	2
6	5	4	7	2	8	3	9	1
5	2	6	8	1	4	9	3	7
9	4	7	3	5	2	1	8	6
3	1	8	9	6	7	2	4	5

135

9	4	6	2	3	1	5	7	8
8	5	1	6	7	4	2	3	9
3	2	7	5	8	9	4	1	6
5	1	2	7	9	6	3	8	4
4	7	3	8	1	5	9	6	2
6	8	9	4	2	3	1	5	7
7	3	8	9	5	2	6	4	1
1	9	4	3	6	8	7	2	5
2	6	5	1	4	7	8	9	3

136

5	4	6	9	1	7	8	3	2
7	2	1	8	3	5	4	9	6
9	3	8	4	2	6	5	7	1
2	6	9	5	8	1	3	4	7
3	1	4	7	6	9	2	8	5
8	5	7	2	4	3	1	6	9
4	7	2	1	9	8	6	5	3
1	9	3	6	5	4	7	2	8
6	8	5	3	7	2	9	1	4

137

5	7	6	3	1	4	8	9	2
8	2	3	5	9	6	7	4	1
1	4	9	2	8	7	3	5	6
7	5	8	9	4	2	1	6	3
9	6	4	8	3	1	2	7	5
3	1	2	7	6	5	4	8	9
4	3	7	6	2	9	5	1	8
6	8	1	4	5	3	9	2	7
2	9	5	1	7	8	6	3	4

138

5	3	8	9	4	2	7	1	6
6	2	1	5	7	3	9	8	4
9	4	7	8	1	6	3	5	2
2	8	3	6	5	1	4	7	9
4	6	9	7	3	8	5	2	1
1	7	5	2	9	4	8	6	3
3	5	6	4	2	7	1	9	8
8	9	4	1	6	5	2	3	7
7	1	2	3	8	9	6	4	5

139

5	3	9	7	4	6	1	8	2
8	6	2	1	9	5	4	7	3
7	4	1	8	3	2	5	6	9
2	8	4	6	5	9	3	1	7
6	1	5	3	8	7	2	9	4
9	7	3	4	2	1	6	5	8
4	9	6	5	7	3	8	2	1
3	5	7	2	1	8	9	4	6
1	2	8	9	6	4	7	3	5

140

8	1	6	2	5	3	7	9	4
9	3	2	1	4	7	8	6	5
4	5	7	6	8	9	3	1	2
2	9	1	3	7	4	5	8	6
7	8	5	9	2	6	1	4	3
3	6	4	8	1	5	2	7	9
6	7	9	5	3	1	4	2	8
5	4	8	7	9	2	6	3	1
1	2	3	4	6	8	9	5	7

141

3	2	1	9	7	8	4	6	5
6	8	7	5	4	2	9	3	1
4	9	5	6	3	1	2	7	8
1	5	6	4	2	9	7	8	3
8	3	2	1	5	7	6	9	4
7	4	9	8	6	3	5	1	2
5	6	3	7	1	4	8	2	9
9	1	4	2	8	6	3	5	7
2	7	8	3	9	5	1	4	6

142

9	2	4	5	8	6	3	1	7
6	5	1	9	7	3	4	8	2
3	7	8	2	1	4	5	6	9
7	3	9	8	5	1	6	2	4
4	8	6	3	2	7	9	5	1
5	1	2	6	4	9	7	3	8
8	6	3	7	9	2	1	4	5
1	9	5	4	6	8	2	7	3
2	4	7	1	3	5	8	9	6

143

7	4	6	8	5	3	2	1	9
3	2	9	4	1	7	6	8	5
5	8	1	6	9	2	4	7	3
8	9	2	1	4	5	7	3	6
1	7	3	2	6	9	5	4	8
6	5	4	7	3	8	1	9	2
4	3	8	5	7	6	9	2	1
2	6	7	9	8	1	3	5	4
9	1	5	3	2	4	8	6	7

144

9	1	4	5	8	3	6	2	7
6	5	2	9	1	7	3	8	4
3	8	7	2	4	6	1	5	9
4	3	9	8	6	5	2	7	1
8	6	1	7	2	4	5	9	3
2	7	5	1	3	9	8	4	6
5	4	8	3	9	1	7	6	2
7	9	3	6	5	2	4	1	8
1	2	6	4	7	8	9	3	5

145

9	7	2	6	3	1	4	5	8
6	4	3	8	5	9	1	7	2
1	8	5	2	4	7	3	9	6
4	2	8	5	9	3	6	1	7
7	1	9	4	6	2	5	8	3
3	5	6	7	1	8	2	4	9
8	3	4	1	7	6	9	2	5
2	9	1	3	8	5	7	6	4
5	6	7	9	2	4	8	3	1

146

9	4	1	3	7	6	8	2	5
8	5	2	1	9	4	6	3	7
6	7	3	5	8	2	1	4	9
4	9	7	6	2	3	5	8	1
2	6	8	7	1	5	3	9	4
3	1	5	8	4	9	7	6	2
1	2	6	4	3	7	9	5	8
7	3	9	2	5	8	4	1	6
5	8	4	9	6	1	2	7	3

147

9	6	7	4	5	2	8	3	1
4	2	1	8	6	3	7	5	9
8	3	5	9	1	7	4	6	2
2	5	6	7	3	1	9	4	8
1	8	4	5	2	9	6	7	3
3	7	9	6	8	4	2	1	5
7	1	2	3	4	8	5	9	6
6	4	3	2	9	5	1	8	7
5	9	8	1	7	6	3	2	4

148

3	9	2	1	7	4	6	5	8
6	8	4	3	5	2	9	1	7
1	7	5	8	9	6	4	3	2
7	6	9	4	3	5	8	2	1
2	4	8	7	6	1	5	9	3
5	1	3	2	8	9	7	6	4
8	5	1	9	2	7	3	4	6
9	2	7	6	4	3	1	8	5
4	3	6	5	1	8	2	7	9

149

6	8	4	2	5	1	3	7	9
7	5	1	9	4	3	6	2	8
9	3	2	8	7	6	5	4	1
3	4	7	1	6	9	2	8	5
1	9	6	5	2	8	4	3	7
8	2	5	7	3	4	1	9	6
4	7	9	6	1	2	8	5	3
5	6	3	4	8	7	9	1	2
2	1	8	3	9	5	7	6	4

150

5	6	3	2	8	4	1	7	9
2	1	4	3	9	7	8	6	5
8	9	7	5	6	1	3	4	2
4	3	5	1	2	8	7	9	6
1	7	9	6	3	5	2	8	4
6	2	8	7	4	9	5	3	1
9	8	1	4	5	3	6	2	7
7	4	6	8	1	2	9	5	3
3	5	2	9	7	6	4	1	8

151

3	1	9	7	2	8	5	6	4
2	7	5	1	6	4	9	3	8
4	8	6	5	9	3	2	1	7
8	4	1	6	5	7	3	2	9
9	3	2	8	4	1	6	7	5
6	5	7	9	3	2	8	4	1
1	9	3	2	7	5	4	8	6
7	6	4	3	8	9	1	5	2
5	2	8	4	1	6	7	9	3

152

4	7	6	8	5	9	2	3	1
3	1	8	6	2	7	4	9	5
9	5	2	3	1	4	8	7	6
5	2	4	7	6	3	9	1	8
6	8	9	2	4	1	7	5	3
7	3	1	5	9	8	6	2	4
8	4	7	9	3	5	1	6	2
1	6	5	4	7	2	3	8	9
2	9	3	1	8	6	5	4	7

153

8	3	5	9	6	1	7	2	4
2	6	7	4	8	3	1	5	9
9	1	4	2	7	5	8	3	6
5	4	9	7	3	2	6	1	8
1	2	3	6	4	8	9	7	5
7	8	6	5	1	9	3	4	2
4	7	8	1	2	6	5	9	3
6	9	1	3	5	4	2	8	7
3	5	2	8	9	7	4	6	1

154

8	1	5	6	9	2	3	4	7
4	2	7	5	8	3	1	6	9
3	6	9	4	7	1	5	8	2
6	4	1	8	5	9	2	7	3
5	7	2	3	1	6	4	9	8
9	3	8	2	4	7	6	5	1
7	9	6	1	2	5	8	3	4
1	8	3	7	6	4	9	2	5
2	5	4	9	3	8	7	1	6

155

4	8	1	5	9	2	3	6	7
5	3	2	7	6	8	9	4	1
9	7	6	3	1	4	5	2	8
8	2	7	9	4	3	1	5	6
1	4	3	2	5	6	7	8	9
6	5	9	8	7	1	4	3	2
7	6	8	1	3	5	2	9	4
2	1	5	4	8	9	6	7	3
3	9	4	6	2	7	8	1	5

156

4	5	1	9	3	8	2	6	7
6	7	8	2	5	4	9	1	3
3	2	9	1	7	6	5	4	8
2	9	7	6	4	5	8	3	1
1	4	6	8	2	3	7	5	9
5	8	3	7	1	9	6	2	4
9	3	4	5	6	7	1	8	2
7	1	5	4	8	2	3	9	6
8	6	2	3	9	1	4	7	5

157

9	2	4	3	5	7	8	6	1
6	3	1	2	8	4	7	5	9
5	7	8	6	1	9	2	3	4
7	8	3	5	9	2	4	1	6
4	5	2	1	6	8	3	9	7
1	9	6	7	4	3	5	8	2
3	6	5	4	2	1	9	7	8
2	1	9	8	7	5	6	4	3
8	4	7	9	3	6	1	2	5

158

2	1	7	8	9	4	5	3	6
8	3	4	1	5	6	2	7	9
5	9	6	3	2	7	8	1	4
9	8	2	5	7	3	6	4	1
6	4	5	2	1	9	7	8	3
3	7	1	4	6	8	9	5	2
1	2	9	7	4	5	3	6	8
4	5	3	6	8	2	1	9	7
7	6	8	9	3	1	4	2	5

159

1	5	3	9	7	6	4	2	8
8	6	2	4	5	1	9	7	3
7	4	9	8	2	3	5	6	1
2	7	8	5	9	4	3	1	6
9	3	6	1	8	2	7	4	5
4	1	5	3	6	7	2	8	9
3	2	4	6	1	9	8	5	7
6	8	7	2	3	5	1	9	4
5	9	1	7	4	8	6	3	2

160

5	3	1	6	9	7	8	2	4
4	6	2	3	5	8	7	1	9
7	9	8	2	1	4	5	3	6
6	4	7	1	8	5	2	9	3
8	1	9	7	3	2	4	6	5
2	5	3	4	6	9	1	7	8
1	7	6	8	4	3	9	5	2
9	2	4	5	7	6	3	8	1
3	8	5	9	2	1	6	4	7

161

5	4	3	9	2	1	7	6	8
1	6	8	7	3	5	4	2	9
7	2	9	6	4	8	1	5	3
2	5	4	8	6	3	9	1	7
6	3	7	4	1	9	2	8	5
9	8	1	5	7	2	6	3	4
4	1	5	2	8	7	3	9	6
3	9	6	1	5	4	8	7	2
8	7	2	3	9	6	5	4	1

162

6	7	8	4	9	3	2	1	5
4	5	2	8	1	7	3	6	9
9	3	1	2	6	5	4	7	8
5	9	4	7	3	2	6	8	1
2	6	3	5	8	1	7	9	4
8	1	7	9	4	6	5	3	2
3	4	6	1	2	8	9	5	7
7	8	9	3	5	4	1	2	6
1	2	5	6	7	9	8	4	3

163

6	2	1	9	4	5	8	7	3
7	4	8	6	3	2	5	1	9
5	3	9	8	1	7	4	6	2
4	5	3	1	2	6	9	8	7
2	1	7	4	8	9	6	3	5
9	8	6	7	5	3	2	4	1
1	7	2	5	6	8	3	9	4
8	9	5	3	7	4	1	2	6
3	6	4	2	9	1	7	5	8

164

5	1	7	9	8	2	4	3	6
8	3	6	1	4	5	7	9	2
2	9	4	3	7	6	8	1	5
9	6	8	2	5	4	3	7	1
3	4	1	7	6	9	5	2	8
7	5	2	8	3	1	9	6	4
6	8	3	5	1	7	2	4	9
4	7	9	6	2	8	1	5	3
1	2	5	4	9	3	6	8	7

165

4	1	2	8	6	3	5	7	9
6	3	5	7	2	9	1	8	4
9	8	7	1	4	5	2	6	3
7	9	4	3	1	2	8	5	6
5	2	8	6	9	4	7	3	1
1	6	3	5	7	8	9	4	2
8	4	1	2	5	6	3	9	7
2	5	6	9	3	7	4	1	8
3	7	9	4	8	1	6	2	5

166

6	1	7	3	4	9	8	5	2
5	3	9	8	6	2	4	1	7
8	4	2	1	5	7	3	9	6
9	6	3	5	7	8	1	2	4
4	2	5	6	9	1	7	3	8
7	8	1	2	3	4	5	6	9
1	9	8	4	2	3	6	7	5
3	7	6	9	8	5	2	4	1
2	5	4	7	1	6	9	8	3

167

5	9	2	8	3	7	4	1	6
1	8	4	9	2	6	5	7	3
6	7	3	4	1	5	9	8	2
9	3	1	7	6	4	8	2	5
8	5	7	2	9	3	1	6	4
4	2	6	5	8	1	3	9	7
3	1	5	6	7	8	2	4	9
2	6	8	3	4	9	7	5	1
7	4	9	1	5	2	6	3	8

168

9	3	6	2	8	4	5	7	1
8	4	7	1	3	5	2	9	6
5	2	1	9	7	6	4	3	8
7	8	4	6	1	9	3	5	2
6	1	2	3	5	7	8	4	9
3	5	9	8	4	2	6	1	7
2	7	3	5	6	1	9	8	4
4	6	8	7	9	3	1	2	5
1	9	5	4	2	8	7	6	3

169

2	8	9	7	3	6	1	5	4
3	6	4	2	5	1	7	9	8
5	7	1	9	8	4	3	6	2
6	1	7	5	4	9	8	2	3
4	2	3	8	6	7	9	1	5
9	5	8	3	1	2	4	7	6
8	4	6	1	7	5	2	3	9
1	9	5	4	2	3	6	8	7
7	3	2	6	9	8	5	4	1

170

3	2	4	9	7	6	5	8	1
7	6	9	8	5	1	2	3	4
1	5	8	2	3	4	9	7	6
4	8	7	5	2	9	6	1	3
2	1	5	6	4	3	7	9	8
6	9	3	1	8	7	4	5	2
9	7	6	4	1	8	3	2	5
8	3	2	7	6	5	1	4	9
5	4	1	3	9	2	8	6	7

171

8	3	2	1	5	9	6	7	4
9	4	7	8	2	6	5	1	3
5	6	1	7	4	3	2	8	9
1	5	8	9	3	7	4	6	2
3	2	6	4	8	1	9	5	7
7	9	4	2	6	5	1	3	8
2	1	5	3	9	8	7	4	6
6	8	9	5	7	4	3	2	1
4	7	3	6	1	2	8	9	5

172

2	4	3	9	8	5	1	7	6
7	6	8	4	1	3	9	5	2
1	5	9	6	2	7	8	4	3
8	1	4	2	7	9	3	6	5
6	2	5	1	3	8	4	9	7
9	3	7	5	4	6	2	8	1
3	9	1	7	6	4	5	2	8
5	7	2	8	9	1	6	3	4
4	8	6	3	5	2	7	1	9

173

4	9	8	2	6	3	1	5	7
3	2	7	9	1	5	8	6	4
6	1	5	8	4	7	9	3	2
5	8	9	3	7	4	6	2	1
7	3	1	6	8	2	5	4	9
2	6	4	1	5	9	7	8	3
8	4	3	7	9	6	2	1	5
9	5	6	4	2	1	3	7	8
1	7	2	5	3	8	4	9	6

174

2	6	9	3	1	5	7	4	8
1	4	3	8	7	6	5	9	2
5	7	8	4	9	2	3	1	6
3	8	1	9	6	7	2	5	4
9	5	6	2	3	4	8	7	1
7	2	4	5	8	1	9	6	3
8	1	5	7	4	3	6	2	9
4	3	2	6	5	9	1	8	7
6	9	7	1	2	8	4	3	5

175

6	3	8	2	4	1	7	5	9
4	1	2	5	9	7	3	6	8
5	7	9	6	8	3	4	1	2
2	8	5	9	3	6	1	7	4
1	9	3	4	7	5	8	2	6
7	6	4	8	1	2	9	3	5
3	4	6	7	2	8	5	9	1
8	2	1	3	5	9	6	4	7
9	5	7	1	6	4	2	8	3

176

8	6	4	2	7	3	1	9	5
5	7	9	6	1	8	2	4	3
3	1	2	5	9	4	8	7	6
2	8	7	4	6	5	3	1	9
9	4	6	7	3	1	5	8	2
1	3	5	8	2	9	7	6	4
4	9	3	1	8	2	6	5	7
7	5	1	3	4	6	9	2	8
6	2	8	9	5	7	4	3	1

177

5	7	3	6	9	1	8	2	4
6	1	9	2	4	8	3	5	7
8	4	2	7	3	5	9	6	1
7	3	6	4	8	9	2	1	5
1	9	5	3	2	7	6	4	8
4	2	8	5	1	6	7	3	9
9	6	4	1	7	2	5	8	3
3	5	7	8	6	4	1	9	2
2	8	1	9	5	3	4	7	6

178

4	3	5	2	8	6	1	7	9
1	7	9	5	3	4	6	2	8
2	8	6	7	9	1	4	5	3
9	5	7	3	6	2	8	4	1
8	6	4	1	7	5	3	9	2
3	2	1	9	4	8	5	6	7
5	9	8	4	1	7	2	3	6
7	1	2	6	5	3	9	8	4
6	4	3	8	2	9	7	1	5

179

2	5	9	7	4	6	3	1	8
4	1	6	2	8	3	5	9	7
8	3	7	5	9	1	2	4	6
7	9	3	4	1	5	6	8	2
1	2	4	3	6	8	7	5	9
6	8	5	9	7	2	1	3	4
5	7	8	6	3	9	4	2	1
3	4	1	8	2	7	9	6	5
9	6	2	1	5	4	8	7	3

180

1	7	4	5	6	3	8	9	2
8	2	5	9	1	4	6	3	7
3	9	6	2	7	8	5	1	4
5	1	8	7	4	9	2	6	3
2	4	7	3	5	6	1	8	9
6	3	9	1	8	2	4	7	5
9	6	1	4	3	5	7	2	8
4	8	3	6	2	7	9	5	1
7	5	2	8	9	1	3	4	6

181

5	3	4	2	8	9	1	7	6
2	7	6	5	4	1	3	8	9
8	1	9	3	7	6	5	4	2
1	4	3	6	9	2	7	5	8
9	8	7	1	5	4	2	6	3
6	2	5	7	3	8	4	9	1
4	9	1	8	2	7	6	3	5
3	6	8	4	1	5	9	2	7
7	5	2	9	6	3	8	1	4

182

4	6	3	2	9	7	8	1	5
5	8	1	4	6	3	7	9	2
7	9	2	5	1	8	3	4	6
8	1	6	7	5	2	4	3	9
3	5	9	8	4	1	6	2	7
2	7	4	6	3	9	5	8	1
9	2	5	3	8	6	1	7	4
1	4	8	9	7	5	2	6	3
6	3	7	1	2	4	9	5	8

183

1	6	4	9	5	3	8	2	7
2	8	5	7	1	4	9	3	6
9	3	7	8	6	2	1	4	5
8	5	6	3	7	1	4	9	2
7	2	1	5	4	9	3	6	8
3	4	9	2	8	6	7	5	1
5	1	2	4	9	8	6	7	3
6	9	3	1	2	7	5	8	4
4	7	8	6	3	5	2	1	9

184

5	4	2	6	1	8	9	3	7
9	6	7	2	4	3	1	8	5
8	3	1	7	9	5	6	2	4
6	9	8	3	7	4	5	1	2
1	7	3	9	5	2	8	4	6
4	2	5	8	6	1	7	9	3
3	1	6	5	2	9	4	7	8
7	8	9	4	3	6	2	5	1
2	5	4	1	8	7	3	6	9

185

5	1	8	2	3	4	6	9	7
3	4	6	5	7	9	2	8	1
2	7	9	1	6	8	3	4	5
6	8	4	3	1	5	7	2	9
1	2	3	9	8	7	5	6	4
9	5	7	6	4	2	8	1	3
8	6	5	7	9	1	4	3	2
7	3	1	4	2	6	9	5	8
4	9	2	8	5	3	1	7	6

186

1	9	8	3	5	6	2	4	7
5	4	2	7	1	8	3	9	6
7	3	6	2	4	9	1	8	5
4	8	5	9	2	7	6	3	1
2	6	9	1	3	4	7	5	8
3	1	7	6	8	5	9	2	4
9	2	4	8	7	1	5	6	3
6	5	1	4	9	3	8	7	2
8	7	3	5	6	2	4	1	9

187

6	9	3	4	8	7	1	2	5
4	1	2	3	5	9	8	6	7
5	7	8	2	1	6	3	4	9
2	8	5	6	4	1	9	7	3
9	3	1	5	7	2	4	8	6
7	6	4	9	3	8	5	1	2
3	5	7	8	2	4	6	9	1
8	2	6	1	9	3	7	5	4
1	4	9	7	6	5	2	3	8

188

7	9	6	8	2	3	1	5	4
5	1	8	6	4	9	2	7	3
2	3	4	5	1	7	6	8	9
3	6	7	1	9	4	5	2	8
9	8	5	7	6	2	4	3	1
4	2	1	3	8	5	7	9	6
6	7	2	9	3	1	8	4	5
1	5	3	4	7	8	9	6	2
8	4	9	2	5	6	3	1	7

189

4	1	2	8	3	6	7	5	9
6	8	5	9	2	7	1	3	4
9	7	3	4	5	1	8	2	6
2	9	8	6	1	3	4	7	5
5	4	1	7	9	8	3	6	2
3	6	7	2	4	5	9	1	8
8	3	4	1	6	2	5	9	7
7	5	6	3	8	9	2	4	1
1	2	9	5	7	4	6	8	3

190

6	1	7	5	9	2	8	3	4
3	5	9	8	4	7	1	6	2
8	2	4	3	1	6	5	7	9
5	6	3	9	7	4	2	8	1
1	9	2	6	8	3	7	4	5
4	7	8	1	2	5	6	9	3
7	3	1	4	5	8	9	2	6
2	4	5	7	6	9	3	1	8
9	8	6	2	3	1	4	5	7

191

7	4	1	8	2	3	6	5	9
2	5	6	7	1	9	8	4	3
8	9	3	5	4	6	2	7	1
1	7	8	2	3	4	9	6	5
4	6	2	9	8	5	3	1	7
9	3	5	1	6	7	4	8	2
3	1	4	6	5	2	7	9	8
5	2	7	4	9	8	1	3	6
6	8	9	3	7	1	5	2	4

192

5	7	1	6	8	4	9	3	2
4	6	9	3	7	2	8	1	5
8	2	3	9	1	5	4	6	7
2	5	8	7	3	6	1	9	4
9	3	7	2	4	1	6	5	8
1	4	6	8	5	9	2	7	3
7	9	5	1	2	8	3	4	6
3	1	2	4	6	7	5	8	9
6	8	4	5	9	3	7	2	1

193

8	9	7	3	2	1	6	5	4
6	1	2	4	7	5	9	3	8
5	3	4	8	6	9	1	2	7
2	5	3	9	1	4	7	8	6
9	7	6	2	8	3	4	1	5
1	4	8	6	5	7	3	9	2
7	2	1	5	9	6	8	4	3
3	6	5	1	4	8	2	7	9
4	8	9	7	3	2	5	6	1

194

8	2	1	7	4	5	3	9	6
4	5	7	6	9	3	1	8	2
9	6	3	1	2	8	7	4	5
5	7	6	8	3	9	4	2	1
2	1	8	4	5	6	9	7	3
3	9	4	2	7	1	6	5	8
1	3	2	9	8	7	5	6	4
7	4	5	3	6	2	8	1	9
6	8	9	5	1	4	2	3	7

195

3	6	9	8	4	1	2	7	5
5	7	8	3	2	9	6	4	1
4	1	2	6	7	5	9	8	3
1	8	6	4	5	2	7	3	9
9	2	4	7	3	6	5	1	8
7	5	3	1	9	8	4	2	6
2	4	1	9	6	3	8	5	7
6	3	7	5	8	4	1	9	2
8	9	5	2	1	7	3	6	4

196

1	9	3	6	8	2	7	4	5
7	5	6	4	9	3	8	2	1
8	4	2	5	7	1	6	3	9
3	6	5	1	2	7	4	9	8
2	8	4	3	6	9	5	1	7
9	7	1	8	4	5	3	6	2
6	3	9	2	5	8	1	7	4
4	2	8	7	1	6	9	5	3
5	1	7	9	3	4	2	8	6

197

1	3	8	2	6	9	5	7	4
7	4	9	8	1	5	3	2	6
6	5	2	4	7	3	9	8	1
2	1	6	9	4	8	7	5	3
4	9	5	7	3	2	6	1	8
3	8	7	6	5	1	4	9	2
5	6	1	3	8	7	2	4	9
8	2	3	5	9	4	1	6	7
9	7	4	1	2	6	8	3	5

198

6	1	3	9	5	8	2	7	4
9	5	7	2	1	4	6	3	8
4	2	8	7	3	6	9	5	1
8	4	6	1	9	3	5	2	7
2	7	9	8	4	5	3	1	6
5	3	1	6	2	7	8	4	9
7	6	5	4	8	2	1	9	3
3	9	4	5	6	1	7	8	2
1	8	2	3	7	9	4	6	5

199

5	1	7	2	3	9	4	8	6
4	6	9	7	1	8	5	3	2
8	3	2	6	5	4	9	1	7
7	8	1	4	2	5	6	9	3
6	9	5	1	8	3	7	2	4
3	2	4	9	7	6	1	5	8
9	4	3	8	6	1	2	7	5
1	7	8	5	4	2	3	6	9
2	5	6	3	9	7	8	4	1

200

2	3	5	1	9	7	8	4	6
7	1	6	4	5	8	3	9	2
8	9	4	2	3	6	7	5	1
1	6	7	5	4	9	2	8	3
5	4	2	8	7	3	6	1	9
3	8	9	6	2	1	5	7	4
6	5	3	7	1	4	9	2	8
9	2	1	3	8	5	4	6	7
4	7	8	9	6	2	1	3	5

201

1	9	4	3	5	7	8	6	2
7	6	8	1	9	2	3	5	4
3	2	5	6	8	4	1	9	7
5	8	2	9	1	3	7	4	6
4	1	3	7	6	5	2	8	9
9	7	6	4	2	8	5	1	3
8	3	9	2	4	1	6	7	5
6	5	7	8	3	9	4	2	1
2	4	1	5	7	6	9	3	8

202

1	8	3	9	6	5	7	4	2
2	6	9	8	4	7	5	3	1
7	5	4	2	3	1	9	8	6
4	3	2	5	1	6	8	7	9
9	1	5	3	7	8	2	6	4
8	7	6	4	2	9	1	5	3
6	2	1	7	5	3	4	9	8
3	9	7	1	8	4	6	2	5
5	4	8	6	9	2	3	1	7

203

8	6	5	1	2	3	7	4	9
3	9	4	8	7	5	6	1	2
2	1	7	4	6	9	3	5	8
5	4	8	6	3	1	9	2	7
1	2	6	9	8	7	4	3	5
9	7	3	2	5	4	8	6	1
6	3	1	7	9	2	5	8	4
4	8	9	5	1	6	2	7	3
7	5	2	3	4	8	1	9	6

204

7	8	3	6	5	2	9	4	1
5	2	6	9	4	1	7	8	3
1	4	9	3	8	7	2	6	5
3	5	2	4	1	6	8	9	7
8	6	7	2	3	9	5	1	4
9	1	4	8	7	5	6	3	2
6	7	5	1	9	3	4	2	8
4	9	1	7	2	8	3	5	6
2	3	8	5	6	4	1	7	9

205

3	4	5	9	6	1	7	8	2
7	9	6	2	8	4	3	1	5
8	1	2	5	7	3	9	6	4
4	2	3	6	1	5	8	9	7
6	5	9	7	3	8	4	2	1
1	7	8	4	9	2	6	5	3
5	3	1	8	4	6	2	7	9
2	8	7	3	5	9	1	4	6
9	6	4	1	2	7	5	3	8

206

5	3	9	8	1	7	2	6	4
2	8	1	5	4	6	3	7	9
4	6	7	2	9	3	1	8	5
1	9	2	6	5	4	8	3	7
3	4	8	7	2	9	6	5	1
7	5	6	3	8	1	9	4	2
8	7	5	1	3	2	4	9	6
6	1	4	9	7	8	5	2	3
9	2	3	4	6	5	7	1	8

207

9	2	7	1	4	6	5	8	3
5	1	6	3	2	8	9	4	7
8	4	3	9	7	5	2	6	1
4	5	8	2	6	7	3	1	9
1	3	2	4	8	9	7	5	6
7	6	9	5	1	3	4	2	8
3	8	4	6	9	2	1	7	5
2	7	5	8	3	1	6	9	4
6	9	1	7	5	4	8	3	2

208

7	9	5	4	3	8	2	6	1
2	4	8	5	1	6	3	9	7
6	3	1	2	7	9	4	8	5
4	6	2	1	9	7	8	5	3
8	7	9	6	5	3	1	4	2
5	1	3	8	4	2	6	7	9
1	5	7	3	6	4	9	2	8
3	2	6	9	8	5	7	1	4
9	8	4	7	2	1	5	3	6

209

7	9	2	8	1	5	3	4	6
3	1	5	7	4	6	2	9	8
8	6	4	2	3	9	5	7	1
1	5	6	3	8	7	4	2	9
2	3	9	6	5	4	8	1	7
4	8	7	9	2	1	6	5	3
9	2	8	4	7	3	1	6	5
6	4	1	5	9	8	7	3	2
5	7	3	1	6	2	9	8	4

210

3	7	1	8	4	2	5	9	6
4	8	2	6	5	9	3	7	1
6	9	5	3	7	1	8	2	4
8	6	7	5	9	3	4	1	2
9	2	4	1	6	8	7	3	5
5	1	3	7	2	4	6	8	9
2	5	8	9	3	6	1	4	7
1	4	6	2	8	7	9	5	3
7	3	9	4	1	5	2	6	8

211

9	3	4	6	1	5	8	7	2
7	5	8	3	2	4	1	6	9
2	1	6	9	8	7	5	3	4
1	6	2	8	4	9	3	5	7
8	7	9	5	6	3	4	2	1
3	4	5	1	7	2	9	8	6
6	2	1	4	3	8	7	9	5
5	8	7	2	9	1	6	4	3
4	9	3	7	5	6	2	1	8

212

7	6	2	9	4	8	5	1	3
5	9	3	7	2	1	8	4	6
1	8	4	3	6	5	9	2	7
2	4	7	1	8	9	6	3	5
8	1	5	6	7	3	4	9	2
6	3	9	4	5	2	1	7	8
9	5	6	2	1	7	3	8	4
4	7	1	8	3	6	2	5	9
3	2	8	5	9	4	7	6	1

213

8	9	7	2	4	1	3	6	5
4	3	2	5	6	7	9	8	1
5	6	1	3	9	8	7	2	4
9	7	4	8	2	3	5	1	6
1	8	3	6	5	9	4	7	2
6	2	5	1	7	4	8	9	3
7	4	6	9	1	5	2	3	8
3	1	9	4	8	2	6	5	7
2	5	8	7	3	6	1	4	9

214

9	7	3	8	1	4	5	6	2
6	2	4	7	3	5	1	9	8
5	8	1	6	2	9	3	4	7
8	3	9	5	4	7	6	2	1
7	6	2	3	9	1	4	8	5
1	4	5	2	8	6	9	7	3
2	1	6	4	5	8	7	3	9
4	9	8	1	7	3	2	5	6
3	5	7	9	6	2	8	1	4

215

2	7	5	9	6	1	8	4	3
9	6	1	8	4	3	7	5	2
4	8	3	5	2	7	9	6	1
6	1	7	4	8	9	2	3	5
8	4	2	7	3	5	1	9	6
5	3	9	2	1	6	4	8	7
1	2	4	6	5	8	3	7	9
7	5	8	3	9	2	6	1	4
3	9	6	1	7	4	5	2	8

216

8	1	3	2	5	7	6	4	9
7	4	5	9	3	6	8	1	2
9	6	2	8	4	1	5	7	3
6	2	4	5	8	3	7	9	1
1	9	7	4	6	2	3	5	8
5	3	8	1	7	9	2	6	4
3	5	9	6	2	4	1	8	7
2	8	1	7	9	5	4	3	6
4	7	6	3	1	8	9	2	5

217

4	3	2	6	1	9	5	7	8
7	8	6	2	5	4	1	3	9
9	1	5	3	7	8	6	4	2
5	7	3	4	2	6	8	9	1
6	9	1	7	8	3	2	5	4
2	4	8	1	9	5	7	6	3
3	5	4	8	6	1	9	2	7
8	6	7	9	3	2	4	1	5
1	2	9	5	4	7	3	8	6

218

8	9	3	5	7	4	6	1	2
1	4	5	3	6	2	7	8	9
6	2	7	1	8	9	4	5	3
7	6	1	2	3	5	8	9	4
9	8	2	7	4	1	3	6	5
5	3	4	6	9	8	2	7	1
3	5	9	8	2	6	1	4	7
2	1	6	4	5	7	9	3	8
4	7	8	9	1	3	5	2	6

219

7	8	6	2	5	4	3	1	9
4	3	5	1	7	9	8	2	6
9	1	2	8	6	3	4	7	5
8	4	1	9	3	6	7	5	2
5	2	3	4	1	7	6	9	8
6	7	9	5	8	2	1	3	4
1	9	4	3	2	8	5	6	7
3	6	8	7	9	5	2	4	1
2	5	7	6	4	1	9	8	3

220

7	1	5	9	2	6	3	4	8
4	8	9	1	7	3	5	2	6
2	3	6	8	4	5	9	1	7
1	7	3	2	8	9	6	5	4
6	5	2	4	3	7	8	9	1
8	9	4	6	5	1	7	3	2
3	6	8	5	1	4	2	7	9
5	2	1	7	9	8	4	6	3
9	4	7	3	6	2	1	8	5

221

9	5	7	8	1	3	4	6	2
6	2	4	5	7	9	1	3	8
1	8	3	4	6	2	5	9	7
2	4	1	6	9	8	3	7	5
8	7	6	3	2	5	9	4	1
3	9	5	1	4	7	2	8	6
4	3	2	7	5	6	8	1	9
7	1	9	2	8	4	6	5	3
5	6	8	9	3	1	7	2	4

222

7	6	1	4	9	2	3	5	8
4	2	9	5	3	8	1	7	6
5	8	3	6	7	1	9	2	4
2	1	4	7	6	5	8	3	9
8	9	6	3	2	4	5	1	7
3	5	7	8	1	9	4	6	2
1	7	2	9	8	3	6	4	5
6	4	8	1	5	7	2	9	3
9	3	5	2	4	6	7	8	1

223

3	8	9	5	4	6	7	2	1
4	5	1	7	8	2	3	9	6
7	6	2	1	9	3	8	5	4
8	4	7	9	6	5	2	1	3
2	9	3	8	1	7	6	4	5
6	1	5	3	2	4	9	8	7
1	2	4	6	7	9	5	3	8
9	3	6	4	5	8	1	7	2
5	7	8	2	3	1	4	6	9

224

8	2	9	1	5	6	7	3	4
3	7	6	9	8	4	5	2	1
1	5	4	3	7	2	6	9	8
6	9	1	7	4	5	2	8	3
2	8	7	6	3	9	4	1	5
4	3	5	8	2	1	9	6	7
9	4	3	5	6	8	1	7	2
5	6	8	2	1	7	3	4	9
7	1	2	4	9	3	8	5	6

225

3	4	7	6	2	9	8	1	5
6	1	8	3	5	4	2	7	9
5	9	2	1	7	8	4	3	6
4	3	5	7	9	1	6	8	2
2	8	6	5	4	3	7	9	1
9	7	1	2	8	6	5	4	3
1	2	4	9	6	7	3	5	8
7	5	9	8	3	2	1	6	4
8	6	3	4	1	5	9	2	7

226

8	7	6	5	1	9	4	2	3
4	9	3	8	2	7	6	5	1
5	1	2	3	6	4	9	7	8
3	5	7	1	9	6	8	4	2
9	2	8	7	4	3	5	1	6
1	6	4	2	5	8	3	9	7
6	8	5	9	7	1	2	3	4
7	3	9	4	8	2	1	6	5
2	4	1	6	3	5	7	8	9

227

2	3	5	1	6	9	7	8	4
1	4	8	5	3	7	9	6	2
9	7	6	8	2	4	5	3	1
3	9	1	4	5	2	8	7	6
8	6	7	9	1	3	4	2	5
5	2	4	6	7	8	3	1	9
4	5	3	2	8	6	1	9	7
6	8	9	7	4	1	2	5	3
7	1	2	3	9	5	6	4	8

228

7	4	1	3	6	5	9	8	2
2	6	5	8	9	4	1	3	7
8	3	9	1	7	2	6	5	4
9	8	3	5	1	7	2	4	6
5	2	7	9	4	6	8	1	3
6	1	4	2	8	3	7	9	5
4	9	6	7	5	1	3	2	8
3	5	8	6	2	9	4	7	1
1	7	2	4	3	8	5	6	9

229

3	6	4	2	8	5	1	7	9
5	2	1	3	9	7	6	4	8
8	7	9	1	6	4	2	5	3
6	8	2	4	5	3	9	1	7
1	9	5	7	2	8	3	6	4
7	4	3	6	1	9	5	8	2
4	5	7	9	3	6	8	2	1
2	3	6	8	7	1	4	9	5
9	1	8	5	4	2	7	3	6

230

9	4	3	8	6	7	5	2	1
5	6	7	1	3	2	4	8	9
8	2	1	5	9	4	6	7	3
6	8	2	4	7	1	3	9	5
1	7	9	3	5	8	2	6	4
3	5	4	9	2	6	8	1	7
2	1	8	7	4	3	9	5	6
7	3	5	6	8	9	1	4	2
4	9	6	2	1	5	7	3	8

231

3	1	5	7	4	8	6	9	2
7	2	8	9	1	6	3	4	5
6	9	4	3	5	2	8	7	1
1	3	9	4	2	5	7	8	6
5	7	6	8	3	1	4	2	9
8	4	2	6	9	7	1	5	3
2	8	3	1	7	9	5	6	4
9	6	1	5	8	4	2	3	7
4	5	7	2	6	3	9	1	8

232

7	6	5	3	1	8	9	4	2
8	3	2	9	6	4	1	5	7
1	9	4	7	2	5	3	8	6
6	5	9	8	3	2	4	7	1
2	7	1	5	4	9	6	3	8
3	4	8	6	7	1	2	9	5
9	2	7	1	8	3	5	6	4
5	1	6	4	9	7	8	2	3
4	8	3	2	5	6	7	1	9

233

4	7	5	2	1	9	6	8	3
2	6	9	8	3	7	4	5	1
1	8	3	5	6	4	7	2	9
6	5	8	7	9	2	3	1	4
7	1	2	3	4	6	8	9	5
9	3	4	1	8	5	2	6	7
8	2	7	4	5	1	9	3	6
3	9	1	6	7	8	5	4	2
5	4	6	9	2	3	1	7	8

234

8	4	1	3	7	9	6	2	5
5	2	9	6	1	4	8	3	7
3	7	6	5	2	8	4	9	1
6	5	8	7	3	2	9	1	4
4	3	7	1	9	6	5	8	2
9	1	2	4	8	5	3	7	6
2	9	4	8	5	1	7	6	3
7	8	5	2	6	3	1	4	9
1	6	3	9	4	7	2	5	8

235

9	6	7	2	3	8	1	4	5
2	1	5	4	9	6	8	7	3
4	8	3	5	7	1	9	6	2
8	9	2	7	6	5	3	1	4
7	5	4	1	8	3	2	9	6
1	3	6	9	2	4	7	5	8
3	4	1	8	5	7	6	2	9
6	7	9	3	4	2	5	8	1
5	2	8	6	1	9	4	3	7

236

3	5	7	6	2	9	4	8	1
6	8	4	7	1	3	2	5	9
2	1	9	5	8	4	3	7	6
8	6	2	3	9	5	1	4	7
9	7	3	8	4	1	6	2	5
1	4	5	2	7	6	9	3	8
4	3	6	1	5	7	8	9	2
7	2	1	9	3	8	5	6	4
5	9	8	4	6	2	7	1	3

237

7	8	6	4	9	1	2	3	5
9	3	4	8	2	5	7	6	1
5	1	2	3	7	6	4	8	9
2	9	7	6	3	8	1	5	4
3	6	5	1	4	2	8	9	7
8	4	1	9	5	7	6	2	3
4	7	8	5	6	9	3	1	2
1	2	9	7	8	3	5	4	6
6	5	3	2	1	4	9	7	8

238

1	5	7	3	9	4	6	8	2
3	9	6	5	8	2	7	4	1
4	2	8	1	7	6	9	5	3
8	4	2	9	6	7	1	3	5
7	3	9	2	5	1	4	6	8
5	6	1	8	4	3	2	9	7
9	7	5	4	2	8	3	1	6
2	8	3	6	1	9	5	7	4
6	1	4	7	3	5	8	2	9

239

2	5	6	3	8	7	4	1	9
9	7	4	5	6	1	3	8	2
1	3	8	2	4	9	5	7	6
6	4	5	7	9	3	1	2	8
7	2	1	8	5	6	9	3	4
3	8	9	4	1	2	7	6	5
4	9	2	1	7	8	6	5	3
8	6	7	9	3	5	2	4	1
5	1	3	6	2	4	8	9	7

240

1	6	8	7	3	9	2	4	5
9	3	4	8	5	2	1	7	6
5	7	2	4	1	6	3	9	8
2	9	6	3	8	4	5	1	7
7	5	3	9	6	1	8	2	4
4	8	1	5	2	7	6	3	9
3	2	7	6	9	5	4	8	1
6	1	9	2	4	8	7	5	3
8	4	5	1	7	3	9	6	2

241

7	4	9	2	3	8	5	6	1
3	8	2	6	1	5	7	4	9
1	6	5	7	9	4	8	2	3
4	3	8	9	5	1	2	7	6
5	7	1	8	6	2	3	9	4
9	2	6	3	4	7	1	5	8
2	1	3	4	7	9	6	8	5
8	5	4	1	2	6	9	3	7
6	9	7	5	8	3	4	1	2

242

1	5	9	3	7	4	2	8	6
8	3	4	2	6	9	1	5	7
7	2	6	8	5	1	3	9	4
5	8	3	4	1	2	6	7	9
6	9	2	7	3	8	4	1	5
4	1	7	6	9	5	8	3	2
2	7	5	1	8	6	9	4	3
9	4	8	5	2	3	7	6	1
3	6	1	9	4	7	5	2	8

243

3	5	1	7	4	6	9	2	8
4	2	6	9	8	5	3	7	1
7	9	8	3	2	1	5	6	4
8	1	5	2	7	3	6	4	9
6	4	3	5	9	8	2	1	7
2	7	9	6	1	4	8	5	3
5	6	7	4	3	9	1	8	2
1	3	4	8	5	2	7	9	6
9	8	2	1	6	7	4	3	5

244

9	4	6	5	1	8	3	7	2
5	1	3	2	7	4	6	9	8
2	8	7	9	6	3	5	1	4
1	6	5	7	9	2	4	8	3
4	3	2	8	5	1	9	6	7
8	7	9	3	4	6	2	5	1
3	5	8	1	2	9	7	4	6
7	2	4	6	8	5	1	3	9
6	9	1	4	3	7	8	2	5

245

7	6	2	9	8	4	1	5	3
3	8	4	5	2	1	7	6	9
9	5	1	7	3	6	2	8	4
5	7	3	1	4	2	6	9	8
1	2	6	3	9	8	5	4	7
4	9	8	6	7	5	3	2	1
8	4	7	2	6	3	9	1	5
2	1	9	8	5	7	4	3	6
6	3	5	4	1	9	8	7	2

246

3	9	7	5	4	8	6	1	2
8	4	6	1	9	2	7	5	3
5	2	1	3	6	7	4	9	8
6	1	3	9	2	5	8	7	4
9	7	2	4	8	1	5	3	6
4	8	5	7	3	6	1	2	9
2	5	9	8	7	4	3	6	1
1	6	4	2	5	3	9	8	7
7	3	8	6	1	9	2	4	5

247

2	5	6	8	4	3	9	1	7
4	1	3	9	6	7	2	5	8
7	9	8	5	1	2	4	3	6
3	8	1	6	7	9	5	4	2
5	2	7	4	3	1	8	6	9
6	4	9	2	8	5	3	7	1
8	7	5	3	9	6	1	2	4
1	3	4	7	2	8	6	9	5
9	6	2	1	5	4	7	8	3

248

9	5	3	8	7	6	1	4	2
4	8	7	9	2	1	5	6	3
6	2	1	5	3	4	8	9	7
8	3	2	4	5	7	9	1	6
1	6	4	3	9	2	7	5	8
5	7	9	1	6	8	3	2	4
7	1	6	2	8	9	4	3	5
3	9	8	6	4	5	2	7	1
2	4	5	7	1	3	6	8	9

249

3	1	4	2	5	6	8	9	7
2	5	9	7	4	8	6	1	3
6	8	7	3	1	9	4	5	2
4	2	8	6	9	1	7	3	5
7	6	5	4	3	2	9	8	1
9	3	1	5	8	7	2	4	6
5	7	3	9	6	4	1	2	8
1	9	2	8	7	3	5	6	4
8	4	6	1	2	5	3	7	9

250

8	2	1	7	6	4	9	3	5
7	9	6	3	5	2	4	8	1
4	3	5	8	9	1	6	2	7
1	8	7	5	4	6	2	9	3
3	5	2	1	8	9	7	4	6
6	4	9	2	3	7	5	1	8
2	1	8	4	7	5	3	6	9
9	7	3	6	2	8	1	5	4
5	6	4	9	1	3	8	7	2

251

9	8	1	7	6	5	3	2	4
7	4	6	8	2	3	9	5	1
2	5	3	1	9	4	8	6	7
5	7	9	4	3	6	2	1	8
1	3	2	5	8	9	7	4	6
8	6	4	2	1	7	5	3	9
4	1	5	9	7	2	6	8	3
6	2	7	3	4	8	1	9	5
3	9	8	6	5	1	4	7	2

252

7	5	2	6	4	1	3	9	8
1	6	3	9	7	8	5	2	4
4	9	8	2	5	3	7	6	1
9	8	5	3	6	4	1	7	2
3	1	7	8	2	5	9	4	6
2	4	6	1	9	7	8	3	5
6	3	1	4	8	9	2	5	7
8	7	4	5	3	2	6	1	9
5	2	9	7	1	6	4	8	3

253

9	4	8	5	1	7	3	2	6
2	3	6	4	9	8	5	7	1
5	1	7	6	3	2	8	4	9
4	5	2	3	6	1	7	9	8
8	6	1	9	7	4	2	3	5
7	9	3	2	8	5	6	1	4
6	2	4	7	5	9	1	8	3
1	7	5	8	4	3	9	6	2
3	8	9	1	2	6	4	5	7

254

6	7	3	8	4	5	1	2	9
1	9	2	3	6	7	8	5	4
5	8	4	2	1	9	6	3	7
9	3	5	1	7	2	4	6	8
7	2	6	9	8	4	3	1	5
4	1	8	5	3	6	7	9	2
8	6	9	7	5	3	2	4	1
3	5	7	4	2	1	9	8	6
2	4	1	6	9	8	5	7	3

255

8	9	6	1	3	7	2	4	5
5	4	3	2	8	6	7	9	1
2	1	7	5	9	4	3	6	8
1	8	2	7	4	9	6	5	3
7	6	5	8	1	3	9	2	4
9	3	4	6	5	2	1	8	7
6	5	8	3	2	1	4	7	9
4	7	1	9	6	5	8	3	2
3	2	9	4	7	8	5	1	6

256

1	3	4	2	6	7	5	8	9
9	6	8	3	1	5	4	7	2
5	2	7	8	9	4	6	3	1
8	1	6	7	2	3	9	5	4
7	4	5	6	8	9	2	1	3
3	9	2	4	5	1	7	6	8
6	5	3	1	4	2	8	9	7
2	8	1	9	7	6	3	4	5
4	7	9	5	3	8	1	2	6

257

4	3	5	2	7	6	9	1	8
8	7	2	1	9	4	6	3	5
6	9	1	5	3	8	2	7	4
5	1	6	4	2	7	8	9	3
3	4	7	8	5	9	1	6	2
9	2	8	6	1	3	5	4	7
1	5	3	7	6	2	4	8	9
7	6	4	9	8	5	3	2	1
2	8	9	3	4	1	7	5	6

258

3	6	4	9	2	1	8	7	5
8	2	5	4	6	7	9	1	3
1	9	7	3	5	8	6	4	2
5	4	2	6	8	3	1	9	7
6	1	8	5	7	9	3	2	4
7	3	9	1	4	2	5	8	6
9	5	3	2	1	4	7	6	8
4	7	6	8	9	5	2	3	1
2	8	1	7	3	6	4	5	9

259

4	3	5	9	1	6	8	7	2
2	7	9	5	4	8	6	3	1
6	8	1	2	3	7	4	9	5
3	6	7	4	2	9	5	1	8
1	5	4	8	6	3	7	2	9
9	2	8	7	5	1	3	6	4
5	4	6	1	7	2	9	8	3
8	1	3	6	9	4	2	5	7
7	9	2	3	8	5	1	4	6

260

4	3	6	1	9	2	5	8	7
1	8	7	5	6	4	3	9	2
9	2	5	3	8	7	4	1	6
5	9	8	2	1	6	7	4	3
3	1	2	7	4	9	8	6	5
7	6	4	8	3	5	1	2	9
6	5	1	4	2	3	9	7	8
8	7	9	6	5	1	2	3	4
2	4	3	9	7	8	6	5	1

261

3	7	9	2	6	4	1	8	5
4	1	6	5	7	8	2	9	3
5	2	8	3	9	1	4	7	6
9	4	2	8	5	6	3	1	7
8	3	5	9	1	7	6	4	2
1	6	7	4	2	3	8	5	9
2	8	4	7	3	5	9	6	1
6	5	3	1	4	9	7	2	8
7	9	1	6	8	2	5	3	4

262

3	1	9	5	6	7	2	4	8
2	8	7	1	4	3	6	5	9
6	5	4	2	8	9	1	3	7
4	6	3	7	5	8	9	2	1
8	2	5	9	3	1	7	6	4
9	7	1	6	2	4	3	8	5
1	4	2	3	7	5	8	9	6
7	3	8	4	9	6	5	1	2
5	9	6	8	1	2	4	7	3

263

9	5	8	3	2	7	4	6	1
7	3	6	8	4	1	5	9	2
4	2	1	5	6	9	3	8	7
6	8	3	9	1	2	7	5	4
2	7	5	6	3	4	8	1	9
1	4	9	7	8	5	6	2	3
8	9	7	1	5	3	2	4	6
3	6	2	4	9	8	1	7	5
5	1	4	2	7	6	9	3	8

264

7	1	4	6	3	5	9	2	8
6	3	8	2	1	9	4	5	7
9	2	5	8	4	7	6	3	1
8	7	9	4	2	6	3	1	5
4	5	3	7	8	1	2	6	9
1	6	2	5	9	3	7	8	4
2	9	6	1	5	4	8	7	3
5	4	7	3	6	8	1	9	2
3	8	1	9	7	2	5	4	6

265

9	6	4	8	3	2	5	1	7
3	5	8	7	4	1	9	2	6
2	7	1	9	5	6	8	3	4
8	2	5	1	6	4	7	9	3
4	3	7	2	8	9	1	6	5
1	9	6	3	7	5	2	4	8
7	4	9	6	1	8	3	5	2
5	1	3	4	2	7	6	8	9
6	8	2	5	9	3	4	7	1

266

3	7	4	6	1	8	2	9	5
5	6	9	3	2	7	4	8	1
8	2	1	9	5	4	7	3	6
1	3	7	2	8	6	9	5	4
9	4	6	5	7	3	1	2	8
2	5	8	1	4	9	6	7	3
7	1	2	4	3	5	8	6	9
6	8	5	7	9	1	3	4	2
4	9	3	8	6	2	5	1	7

267

2	3	5	9	1	6	4	8	7
7	4	6	5	8	2	1	9	3
9	8	1	3	7	4	5	2	6
3	9	8	7	5	1	2	6	4
1	7	4	6	2	9	8	3	5
5	6	2	4	3	8	7	1	9
6	2	7	1	9	5	3	4	8
4	1	3	8	6	7	9	5	2
8	5	9	2	4	3	6	7	1

268

8	2	6	4	9	1	5	3	7
1	4	7	2	5	3	9	8	6
9	3	5	8	7	6	4	1	2
2	6	1	5	8	7	3	9	4
3	7	9	1	6	4	2	5	8
5	8	4	9	3	2	7	6	1
4	5	8	6	2	9	1	7	3
6	1	3	7	4	5	8	2	9
7	9	2	3	1	8	6	4	5

269

8	4	5	1	2	9	3	6	7
7	1	9	8	3	6	5	4	2
6	3	2	4	7	5	1	8	9
2	8	6	9	1	3	4	7	5
5	9	4	2	6	7	8	3	1
1	7	3	5	8	4	9	2	6
3	2	8	6	9	1	7	5	4
9	5	7	3	4	2	6	1	8
4	6	1	7	5	8	2	9	3

270

4	7	5	2	3	9	1	6	8
6	1	8	5	4	7	3	2	9
3	2	9	1	8	6	7	4	5
9	8	6	4	1	3	2	5	7
5	3	1	6	7	2	9	8	4
7	4	2	9	5	8	6	3	1
1	6	3	8	9	4	5	7	2
2	5	4	7	6	1	8	9	3
8	9	7	3	2	5	4	1	6

271

5	1	6	4	3	8	2	9	7
2	9	8	5	7	1	4	3	6
7	4	3	9	6	2	1	5	8
4	3	5	8	1	9	7	6	2
1	6	2	7	4	3	5	8	9
9	8	7	2	5	6	3	4	1
6	7	4	1	8	5	9	2	3
3	2	1	6	9	4	8	7	5
8	5	9	3	2	7	6	1	4

272

9	6	2	3	5	4	8	1	7
1	8	4	7	9	6	2	5	3
3	7	5	8	2	1	4	9	6
5	2	6	9	3	7	1	4	8
7	9	1	2	4	8	3	6	5
8	4	3	6	1	5	7	2	9
2	5	9	4	7	3	6	8	1
4	3	8	1	6	9	5	7	2
6	1	7	5	8	2	9	3	4

273

7	1	9	3	8	2	4	6	5
6	3	4	7	5	1	8	9	2
2	5	8	6	4	9	3	7	1
3	8	1	5	7	6	9	2	4
4	6	2	9	1	8	7	5	3
5	9	7	4	2	3	6	1	8
9	4	6	1	3	5	2	8	7
8	7	5	2	6	4	1	3	9
1	2	3	8	9	7	5	4	6

274

2	1	7	8	5	3	9	6	4
3	4	9	1	6	7	2	8	5
6	8	5	2	9	4	1	7	3
9	6	1	4	7	5	8	3	2
8	3	4	9	2	1	6	5	7
7	5	2	6	3	8	4	9	1
5	2	8	3	4	6	7	1	9
1	9	3	7	8	2	5	4	6
4	7	6	5	1	9	3	2	8

275

4	1	6	2	7	8	9	5	3
9	8	2	3	5	4	1	7	6
7	3	5	9	6	1	4	2	8
8	9	1	7	3	6	5	4	2
6	7	3	4	2	5	8	9	1
2	5	4	1	8	9	6	3	7
1	2	8	5	9	3	7	6	4
3	4	9	6	1	7	2	8	5
5	6	7	8	4	2	3	1	9

276

4	3	9	7	2	6	8	1	5
2	5	8	4	9	1	7	3	6
7	1	6	3	8	5	2	9	4
6	2	5	8	4	9	3	7	1
1	7	3	6	5	2	4	8	9
9	8	4	1	7	3	6	5	2
3	9	7	2	1	4	5	6	8
8	4	1	5	6	7	9	2	3
5	6	2	9	3	8	1	4	7

277

2	7	5	8	4	6	3	1	9
9	8	6	7	3	1	4	2	5
4	3	1	9	5	2	8	7	6
1	2	9	3	8	5	6	4	7
8	6	4	2	1	7	5	9	3
3	5	7	6	9	4	2	8	1
7	9	2	4	6	3	1	5	8
6	1	8	5	2	9	7	3	4
5	4	3	1	7	8	9	6	2

278

1	9	3	5	4	8	6	2	7
5	2	8	6	3	7	4	1	9
4	6	7	1	9	2	8	5	3
6	8	5	3	2	4	7	9	1
9	7	1	8	5	6	3	4	2
2	3	4	9	7	1	5	6	8
7	1	9	4	6	3	2	8	5
3	5	6	2	8	9	1	7	4
8	4	2	7	1	5	9	3	6

279

3	7	6	4	9	5	8	1	2
4	1	9	6	2	8	7	5	3
5	8	2	1	3	7	6	9	4
7	2	3	5	8	1	4	6	9
9	5	8	2	4	6	3	7	1
1	6	4	9	7	3	5	2	8
8	9	5	3	6	2	1	4	7
6	4	7	8	1	9	2	3	5
2	3	1	7	5	4	9	8	6

280

9	2	8	4	5	6	3	1	7
3	5	4	7	1	2	8	6	9
6	7	1	3	8	9	5	4	2
5	6	3	2	9	1	4	7	8
4	8	9	6	7	3	2	5	1
7	1	2	8	4	5	9	3	6
2	4	6	1	3	8	7	9	5
1	9	7	5	2	4	6	8	3
8	3	5	9	6	7	1	2	4

281

7	3	5	2	6	4	1	8	9
1	6	9	7	8	3	4	2	5
8	2	4	9	5	1	7	3	6
4	9	1	8	2	6	5	7	3
6	5	7	3	4	9	8	1	2
3	8	2	5	1	7	9	6	4
2	1	6	4	9	8	3	5	7
5	4	3	1	7	2	6	9	8
9	7	8	6	3	5	2	4	1

282

9	7	8	3	5	1	6	2	4
5	3	2	4	6	9	1	8	7
1	4	6	7	2	8	5	3	9
8	6	3	9	4	2	7	1	5
4	5	9	1	7	3	2	6	8
2	1	7	6	8	5	9	4	3
7	2	1	5	3	4	8	9	6
6	9	4	8	1	7	3	5	2
3	8	5	2	9	6	4	7	1

283

2	9	4	5	6	8	1	3	7
8	7	3	1	9	2	5	4	6
6	5	1	7	4	3	9	8	2
3	6	8	4	5	9	7	2	1
9	1	5	2	3	7	4	6	8
4	2	7	8	1	6	3	9	5
7	3	9	6	8	1	2	5	4
5	8	2	9	7	4	6	1	3
1	4	6	3	2	5	8	7	9

284

8	3	4	2	7	1	9	5	6
2	5	6	3	8	9	4	7	1
9	1	7	4	6	5	3	8	2
6	9	3	7	2	8	1	4	5
7	8	1	5	3	4	2	6	9
5	4	2	1	9	6	8	3	7
1	7	5	8	4	2	6	9	3
4	2	9	6	5	3	7	1	8
3	6	8	9	1	7	5	2	4

285

5	9	6	2	4	7	8	3	1
3	1	8	5	6	9	7	4	2
4	7	2	3	8	1	9	5	6
8	6	5	1	7	2	3	9	4
7	3	1	6	9	4	5	2	8
2	4	9	8	3	5	6	1	7
9	2	4	7	5	6	1	8	3
6	5	3	4	1	8	2	7	9
1	8	7	9	2	3	4	6	5

286

9	2	7	3	6	8	4	1	5
3	5	6	2	4	1	7	8	9
8	1	4	5	9	7	2	6	3
6	7	3	4	1	5	9	2	8
2	4	9	8	7	6	3	5	1
1	8	5	9	3	2	6	4	7
5	9	2	7	8	4	1	3	6
7	6	8	1	2	3	5	9	4
4	3	1	6	5	9	8	7	2

287

5	1	6	2	8	3	4	7	9
9	3	7	1	6	4	2	5	8
2	4	8	5	9	7	6	3	1
1	5	2	7	4	9	3	8	6
7	8	3	6	1	2	9	4	5
4	6	9	8	3	5	1	2	7
3	9	5	4	7	1	8	6	2
8	2	1	3	5	6	7	9	4
6	7	4	9	2	8	5	1	3

288

8	3	6	9	4	5	2	7	1
9	1	4	7	2	3	8	5	6
7	2	5	6	1	8	3	9	4
4	8	9	2	3	7	6	1	5
2	5	3	1	6	4	7	8	9
6	7	1	8	5	9	4	2	3
3	6	2	5	7	1	9	4	8
1	9	7	4	8	6	5	3	2
5	4	8	3	9	2	1	6	7

289

9	3	1	4	8	2	6	7	5
2	4	5	6	7	1	3	8	9
6	7	8	3	5	9	2	4	1
8	6	2	7	4	5	9	1	3
4	9	3	1	2	8	7	5	6
5	1	7	9	6	3	8	2	4
3	5	4	8	9	7	1	6	2
1	8	6	2	3	4	5	9	7
7	2	9	5	1	6	4	3	8

290

2	4	5	7	9	1	6	8	3
6	7	1	8	2	3	4	5	9
3	9	8	4	5	6	7	1	2
4	1	3	2	8	7	5	9	6
5	8	6	3	1	9	2	7	4
9	2	7	5	6	4	1	3	8
7	5	4	9	3	2	8	6	1
1	3	2	6	7	8	9	4	5
8	6	9	1	4	5	3	2	7

291

5	9	1	8	4	2	7	6	3
8	2	4	3	7	6	5	9	1
6	3	7	1	5	9	2	4	8
3	1	5	6	9	4	8	2	7
4	6	2	5	8	7	3	1	9
7	8	9	2	3	1	6	5	4
9	4	6	7	2	3	1	8	5
2	5	3	9	1	8	4	7	6
1	7	8	4	6	5	9	3	2

292

8	3	9	6	1	4	5	7	2
7	2	6	9	5	3	4	1	8
5	4	1	2	7	8	9	3	6
1	8	5	7	4	2	3	6	9
3	7	2	5	6	9	8	4	1
9	6	4	8	3	1	7	2	5
4	5	7	1	9	6	2	8	3
2	1	3	4	8	5	6	9	7
6	9	8	3	2	7	1	5	4

293

1	9	6	3	4	8	2	7	5
8	2	7	5	6	1	4	3	9
4	3	5	9	7	2	1	6	8
3	7	2	1	8	9	6	5	4
5	6	8	4	2	7	3	9	1
9	4	1	6	3	5	7	8	2
6	1	4	8	5	3	9	2	7
7	8	9	2	1	6	5	4	3
2	5	3	7	9	4	8	1	6

294

2	3	1	8	4	6	5	7	9
9	6	5	1	7	2	4	8	3
4	8	7	3	9	5	2	1	6
1	9	4	2	3	7	8	6	5
6	2	3	9	5	8	1	4	7
7	5	8	6	1	4	9	3	2
3	1	6	5	8	9	7	2	4
5	7	2	4	6	1	3	9	8
8	4	9	7	2	3	6	5	1

295

5	1	8	2	6	9	7	4	3
3	9	7	1	5	4	2	6	8
6	4	2	8	7	3	9	1	5
2	7	5	3	4	6	8	9	1
4	3	9	7	8	1	6	5	2
1	8	6	5	9	2	4	3	7
7	6	1	9	2	5	3	8	4
9	2	3	4	1	8	5	7	6
8	5	4	6	3	7	1	2	9

296

7	3	9	2	6	8	5	1	4
6	5	2	1	4	7	9	8	3
8	1	4	3	9	5	6	7	2
9	4	7	6	2	1	8	3	5
1	8	5	7	3	4	2	9	6
2	6	3	8	5	9	1	4	7
5	7	6	9	8	3	4	2	1
4	9	1	5	7	2	3	6	8
3	2	8	4	1	6	7	5	9

297

5	9	8	1	4	2	3	6	7
1	4	2	7	6	3	9	5	8
6	3	7	9	8	5	2	1	4
3	2	9	8	7	6	5	4	1
4	7	6	3	5	1	8	2	9
8	1	5	2	9	4	6	7	3
2	8	4	5	1	9	7	3	6
9	5	1	6	3	7	4	8	2
7	6	3	4	2	8	1	9	5

298

6	4	7	3	5	1	2	8	9
1	5	8	6	2	9	4	3	7
2	3	9	7	4	8	1	5	6
3	7	5	8	6	4	9	2	1
9	2	1	5	7	3	8	6	4
4	8	6	1	9	2	5	7	3
5	6	4	9	8	7	3	1	2
8	9	3	2	1	6	7	4	5
7	1	2	4	3	5	6	9	8

299

7	6	5	1	2	8	3	9	4
3	4	2	5	6	9	7	8	1
9	8	1	3	7	4	2	6	5
8	7	3	4	5	2	6	1	9
6	2	9	8	1	3	5	4	7
1	5	4	6	9	7	8	3	2
2	3	7	9	4	6	1	5	8
5	9	8	7	3	1	4	2	6
4	1	6	2	8	5	9	7	3

300

3	8	1	5	7	2	6	4	9
7	2	9	1	6	4	8	3	5
6	4	5	3	8	9	2	7	1
2	1	8	9	4	6	7	5	3
5	7	3	8	2	1	9	6	4
4	9	6	7	5	3	1	8	2
8	5	4	2	1	7	3	9	6
1	3	7	6	9	5	4	2	8
9	6	2	4	3	8	5	1	7